The Practical Guide to Operating and Maintaining a Delta FDM 3D Printer 2026

Introduction

Different 3D printers have slightly different features. In the world of Fused Deposition Modeling FDM printers, Cartesian and Delta 3D printers are the most popular among hobbyists who are new to 3D printing.

The primary difference between Cartesian and Delta 3D printers lies in how movement is coordinated with the print bed. In a Cartesian printer, particularly the common "bed-slinger" design, the print head can move up and down, but this vertical movement must be carefully coordinated with the movement of the print bed on the Z-plane, meaning the bed itself moves either forward and backward or up and down. This creates a situation where a heavy component, the print bed, is in motion, which can limit speed and cause taller prints to wobble. By contrast, in a Delta printer, the print head can move freely in any direction through the precise coordination of its three angled arms, while the print tray remains completely stationary at all times. Because the bed never moves, Delta printers can achieve much higher speeds and accelerations, though their calibration is more complex and their build volume is typically cylindrical rather than rectangular. The fixed bed design of a Delta contributes to its stability and speed, but it also means the printer relies entirely on complex software calculations to translate coordinated vertical movements of the three arms into smooth horizontal and vertical motion of the print head.

This book covers the essential 3D printing terminologies, with focus on elements that are more relevant to entry level Delta 3D printers. They are written to be more human while being technically accurate and useful. We use a particular 3d printer and software for demo. This book, however, is not meant to be a brand/model specific tutorial.

Restrictions on Alteration and Copying

Table of Contents

Is Delta printer still relevant today?

Delta printers are still relevant today, but they now occupy a more specialized niche rather than serving as the all-purpose solution they were once considered. While Cartesian and CoreXY systems dominate the general consumer market, Delta printers continue to hold their own in specific applications where their unique mechanical advantages shine. The enduring relevance of Delta printers stems primarily from two inherent strengths. First, no other common printer architecture can match their extreme vertical build volume relative to their desktop footprint. Because the print head is suspended from three towers and the bed remains completely stationary, a Delta printer can produce remarkably tall objects while taking up very little space. A machine like the FLSUN S1, for example, offers a build height of 430 millimeters with a circular diameter of 320 millimeters, achieving a vertical range that few comparably priced Cartesian machines can approach. This makes Delta printers exceptional for printing slender, tall items such as cosplay staffs and swords, architectural scale models, vases, busts, and detailed figurines.

Second, Delta kinematics excel at producing smooth curved surfaces. The coordinated motion of the three arms naturally generates exceptionally clean circular and cylindrical paths without the step-like artifacts that can appear on curved surfaces printed by Cartesian machines. This advantage is backed by recent academic research confirming that Delta printers perform measurably better than Cartesian printers when it comes to curved geometries. The lightweight effector also allows for faster acceleration and directional changes with less vibration, which contributes to cleaner surface finishes even at high printing speeds.

However, Delta printers are not without significant limitations. Their circular build area means the usable footprint is smaller than a rectangular bed of comparable diameter, making them inefficient for printing wide, flat objects like panels or trays. Calibration has historically been more complex than with Cartesian printers, though modern machines have largely addressed this with automated calibration systems. Additionally, Delta printers lack the extensive ecosystem support found with popular Cartesian platforms, meaning fewer accessories, smaller user communities, and less ready-made support for multicolor printing systems.

Ultimately, a Delta printer is not the best choice for every user or every application. For general-purpose printing, large flat objects, or those wanting seamless ecosystem integration, a well-calibrated Cartesian or CoreXY printer is likely a better fit. But for users who regularly print tall, slender objects, who prioritize speed and smooth curved surfaces, or who simply appreciate the mechanical elegance and visual appeal of the design, Delta printers remain a uniquely capable and entirely relevant option in the 2026 3D printing landscape.

FDM, Delta and Cartesian

From the context of a user, a plane (aka work plane) is like a table top — it gives you a surface for working.

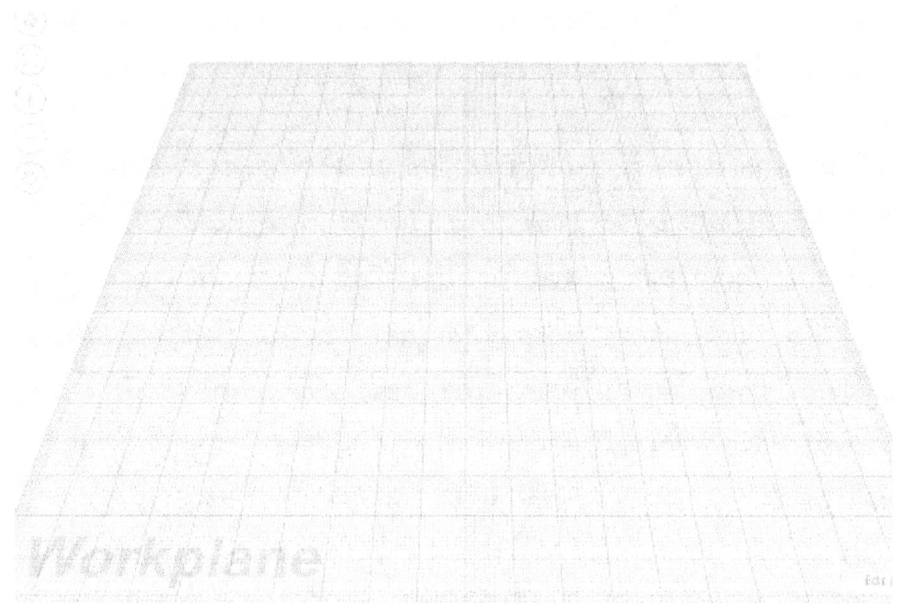

Things "on" a plane can be moved or scaled in multiple directions. Movement on the plane is movement on the Z surface, which is front to back. On the other hand, X is side to side while Y is up and down. **At least this is how things work when you are using your software to create and print a 3D object.**

Cartesian printer has a print bed which moves on the Z plane, along X and Z. Its print head, on the other hand, can move vertically. The good thing about this design is that the print head gets less shaky when operating. However, there are two moving parts, meaning there are more complicated components to be taken care of. It is also quite slow.

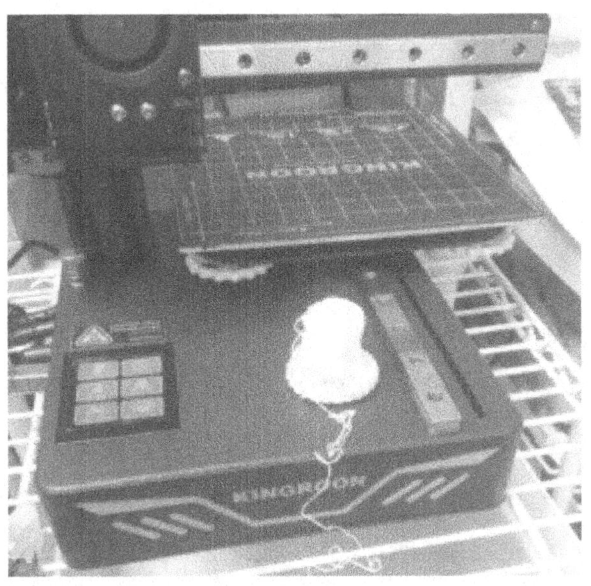

A CoreXY printer also has a cartesian design but the print bed moves vertically, and that the print head moves on both the X and Y axes horizontally.

In reality, the work plane of a Delta printer is not really physical... in fact, the work plane is not a fixed, physical surface like the print bed itself, but rather an imaginary horizontal plane in space where the print head is currently positioned and actively extruding material. To understand this concept properly, one must recognize that a delta printer performs all of its printing within a fully three-dimensional cylindrical workspace, and the work plane is simply the horizontal slice through that cylindrical volume at a particular Z height. At any given moment during a print, the effector moves within a specific work plane, tracing out the two-dimensional pattern of the current layer while remaining at a constant height above the bed.

Even though it is always parallel to the print bed, it is not necessarily flat in a mechanical sense. While the work plane is mathematically flat, representing a constant Z value across all X and Y coordinates, the physical realization of that plane depends entirely on proper calibration of the printer. If the delta printer's endstops are not perfectly set, or if the tower positions are slightly misaligned, the effector will tilt as it moves across the work plane, causing the nozzle to dip or rise at different radial positions. This manifests as inconsistent layer heights, where the work plane becomes effectively warped or tilted even though the firmware believes it is maintaining a constant Z coordinate. For this reason, delta printers require a calibration process. We will talk about this later in this book. And, the circular shape of the delta printer's work plane deserves attention. While a Cartesian printer's work plane is rectangular, matching the shape of its X and Y axes, a delta printer's work plane is a circle whose radius is determined by the length of the arms and the geometry of the towers. The effective work plane is actually slightly smaller than the maximum possible circle, because near the extreme edges the arms approach their mechanical limits and linear motion becomes less accurate. Within the central region of the work plane, where accuracy is highest, the effector moves nearly like a Cartesian machine with excellent isotropy, meaning motion in any horizontal direction has similar dynamic properties. Toward the edge of the circular work plane, however, the motion becomes increasingly anisotropic, with movement parallel to a tower requiring different arm dynamics than movement perpendicular to that tower. A skilled user would always choose the work plane's usable diameter carefully when slicing models, ensuring that all critical features remain within the region where the delta mechanism performs optimally.

For a Delta printer, the print head can move freely on X, Y and Z through coordination among the 3 arms (to be precise, 3 SETS of arms). The arms are driven by belts.

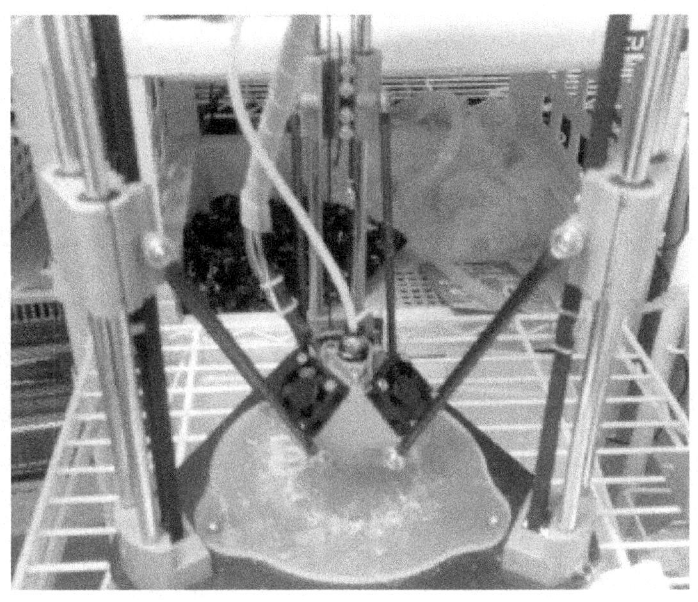

We call this a delta motion mechanism, a form of parallel kinematics that differs fundamentally from the stacked linear axes of a Cartesian printer. Instead of moving a print head along separate X, Y, and Z rails, a delta printer suspends its print head from three independent vertical rails arranged in a triangle. Each rail carries a sliding carriage connected to the central print head, known as the effector, by a pair of parallel rods. These rods form the arms of the mechanism, and their parallel arrangement ensures that the effector remains perfectly level relative to the build platform at all times, preventing it from tilting or rotating as it moves.

To understand how the system creates three-dimensional movement, imagine a circular print bed at the center of the machine. Surrounding this bed are the three vertical rails, typically spaced one hundred twenty degrees apart around the circumference. Each carriage on these rails can slide up and down independently under the control of its own stepper motor. When all three carriages move upward by exactly the same distance at the same speed, the effector rises vertically, creating pure Z-axis movement straight up from the bed. Conversely, when all three carriages descend together, the effector moves down toward the bed.

The magic of delta motion lies in what happens when the carriages move differently from one another. If the carriage on one rail moves down while the other two move up or stay in place, the effector is pulled horizontally toward that descending carriage. By carefully coordinating the relative positions and speeds of all three carriages, the effector can be positioned at any point within a cylindrical volume above the print bed. For example, to move the effector in a straight horizontal line along the X axis, the control software calculates a precise combination of movements for all three carriages simultaneously, none of which individually move in a straight horizontal line. The resulting motion is a complex choreography where each carriage follows its own path, but their combined effect is a smooth, predictable trajectory of the print head through Cartesian space.

This mechanism is governed by mathematical transformations known as forward and inverse kinematics. The inverse kinematics calculation takes a desired X, Y, Z coordinate for the print head and determines exactly how high each of the three carriages must be positioned to achieve that location. The forward kinematics calculation performs the opposite conversion, determining the effector's position from known carriage heights. These calculations are performed hundreds of times per second by the printer's firmware, using the geometry of the machine including arm lengths, tower radius, and effector offset. Small errors in any of these geometric parameters produce visible print defects such as conical warping or non-circular holes, which explains why delta printers have historically required more careful calibration than their Cartesian counterparts.

The mechanical consequences of this design are significant. Because the heavy stepper motors and tracks remain stationary on the vertical rails, and only the lightweight carriages, arms, and effector move during printing, delta mechanisms achieve very low moving mass. This allows for exceptional acceleration and rapid direction changes without the ringing or ghosting artifacts that plague heavy-bed Cartesian machines. However, the use of three arms also creates a trade-off in build volume shape. The usable printing area is circular, with print quality and accuracy degrading near the outer edges where the arms approach their angular limits. The vertical range is excellent, but the horizontal range is constrained by the need to keep the arms within their comfortable operational angles. This fundamental geometry explains why delta printers excel at tall, slender objects but struggle with wide, flat prints that would better suit a rectangular Cartesian bed.

Practically, the problem with this mechanism is that the print head may move too much and get shaky. The wires and tube attached to it may eventually get loose or even break apart. Another thing - most Delta printers do not allow for print bed level adjustment. Many also lack heating for the bed. If you take apart the top of a Delta printer, you will see 4 stepping motors, one at each corner for manipulating a set of arms (via belts), plus one for material loading.

They are brushless DC motors that are highly accurate in movement and positioning. A motor driver circuitry receives signals from the microcontroller and provides electrical current with a voltage suitable and sufficient for driving the motors. The driver circuitry can be configured to move its motor very precisely, like in 1, 1/2, 1/4, 1/8, or 1/16 steps per pulse. And pulse is related to PWM. PWM means PWM pulse width modulation, which is a method of speed control for driving the motor with a series of ON OFF pulses. Varying such duty cycle can effectively control the output. We need PWM and stepping motors since movement of the arms and the material feeding mechanism must be highly precise and accurate. Standard regular DC motors cannot achieve this.

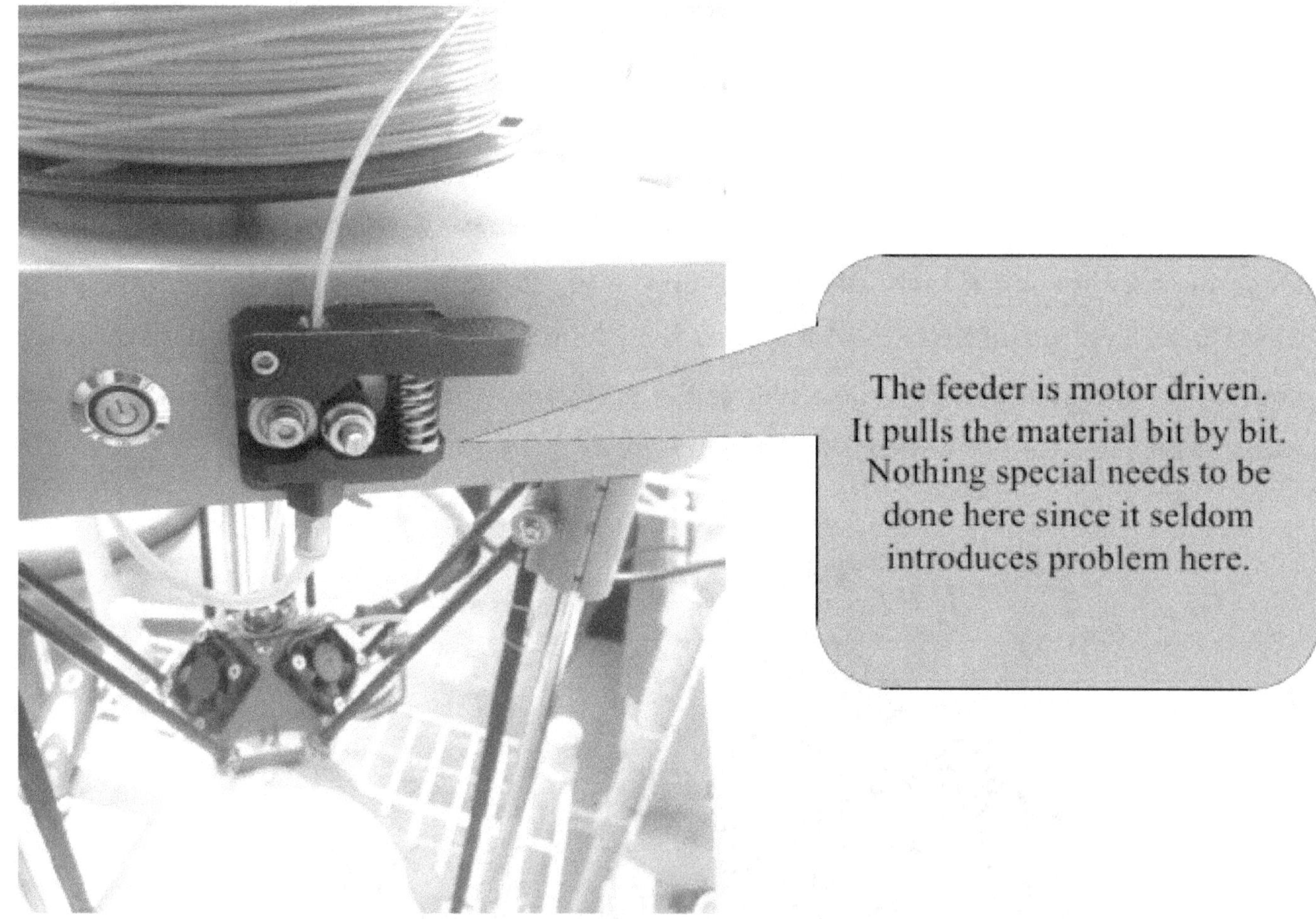

As you can see from the previous photo, the motors are pretty big so they they can afford to work pretty fast. The speed they work at is directly related to the print speed. Most software allows you to adjust the print speed.

We usually care more about the speed related to printing. For the top, bottom, and shell we want a slower print speed so there will be less force applied to the molten material as it is extruded, allowing for better adhesion. The core reasoning is that the molten thermoplastic being extruded from a nozzle behaves like a very viscous fluid. When you print faster, the material is pushed through the nozzle at higher pressure, exits at greater velocity, and is laid down while the print head is moving more quickly across the previous layer. This increased speed applies greater shear forces to the molten material as it is stretched and dragged into place. Slower speeds reduce these forces, giving the material more time to settle, flow into the tiny gaps between itself and the previous layer, and form a strong bond through a process called fusion bonding or polymer chain entanglement across the layer interface. For both the first layer adhering to the build plate and for the outer perimeters that define the part's surface quality and structural integrity, slower speeds genuinely improve adhesion and surface finish.

However, the relationship between speed and adhesion is not purely linear, nor is slower universally better. Every material has an optimal flow rate window determined by its melt viscosity and thermal properties. If you print the top, bottom, and shell too slowly, the material spends too much time in the nozzle and on the print, leading to heat soak, oozing, stringing, and actually weaker layer adhesion because the molten plastic begins to crystallize or degrade before being properly pressed into the previous layer. For example, PLA prints beautifully at moderate to high speeds, but printing its outer shell at extremely slow speeds like five millimeters per second often produces a rough, overheated surface where the material has dragged and blobbing has occurred.

Also, top and bottom layers refer mostly to horizontal surfaces where the extrusion is laid down onto a solid base of previous layers or onto the build plate itself. Shells refer to vertical perimeters that define the outer walls of the part. For vertical shells, the dominant adhesion concern is interlayer adhesion between successive perimeters stacked upward. For top layers, the concern is bridging across sparse infill and achieving a smooth, solid surface without gaps. For bottom layers, the concern is first layer squish and bed adhesion. Each of these will benefit from slower speeds, but for slightly different reasons that depend on geometry, not just on the general concept of reducing force on molten material.

And, infill which by contrast does not need the same level of adhesion because it merely supports the top layers and provides internal structure. Many slicers therefore use separate speed settings, printing infill much faster than the outer perimeters and solid layers. This strategy gives the best of both worlds, structural speed where it does not matter visually or mechanically, and careful slow printing exactly where adhesion and finish are critical.

Non-print move deals with traveling between one extrusion point and another. Technically this should be made as fast as possible so the chance for filament oozing from the nozzle can be kept minimal. However, the simple directive to make travel moves as fast as possible runs into mechanical and firmware limitations. A printer's stepper motors and motion system have maximum acceleration and velocity limits. If travel moves are set too fast, the printer may attempt to move the nozzle faster than the motors can reliably control, leading to skipped steps, layer shifting, or lost position. Even if the motors can reach the commanded speed, the sudden deceleration at the end of an extremely fast travel move can cause the machine to shake or vibrate, possibly disturbing the print or creating visible ringing artifacts on nearby surfaces. Modern firmware implements jerk and acceleration control to smooth these transitions, but there is still a practical upper bound beyond which faster travel speeds stop improving quality and start causing new problems.

Another nuance involves the relationship between travel speed and oozing mitigation. While very fast travel moves do reduce oozing time, they also create a more aggressive yanking motion on the oozing filament as the nozzle accelerates away from the previous extrusion point and decelerates upon arrival. In some cases, a moderately fast but smooth travel move with controlled acceleration produces less stringing than an extremely fast travel move with sharp starts and stops, because the sudden acceleration can snap an oozing string rather than allowing it to form gradually. Many experienced users therefore set travel speeds to something like one hundred fifty to two hundred fifty millimeters per second, which is fast enough to minimize oozing but not so aggressive that the printer shakes violently or the filament behaves unpredictably.

Furthermore, modern printing has introduced alternative strategies that reduce or eliminate the need for blazingly fast travel moves. Some printers and firmware support linear advance or pressure advance, which actively retracts or decompresses filament at the end of an extrusion segment, reducing the residual pressure that causes oozing in the first place. If retraction is tuned well and pressure is properly managed, the nozzle will barely ooze at all even during slow travel moves. Similarly, technologies like "wipe" and "coast" move the nozzle slightly while reducing extrusion pressure before a travel move, further minimizing the available molten material to ooze. With these features active, the difference between moderately fast and extremely fast travel speeds becomes much less significant for stringing prevention. And, certain materials and geometries would require careful travel speed tuning rather than simply maximizing speed. Flexible filaments like TPU are notorious for being sensitive to acceleration and speed changes, and extremely fast travel moves can cause the filament to buckle in the extruder or produce inconsistent retraction behavior.

Do note that for a Delta printer, moving too fast may lead to a shaky print head. The belts that control the arms can get loosen easily. So are the wires attached to the print head.

Slicer and Cura

Regardless of the type of printer you use, the slicer still works the same. Your slicer software would allow you to move and rotate your object along X, Y or Z, allowing you to determine the print position relative to the print bed. Some even allow you to scale or mirror your object right before printing. How the 3D printer implements the model and performs the printing is not something you need to worry about.

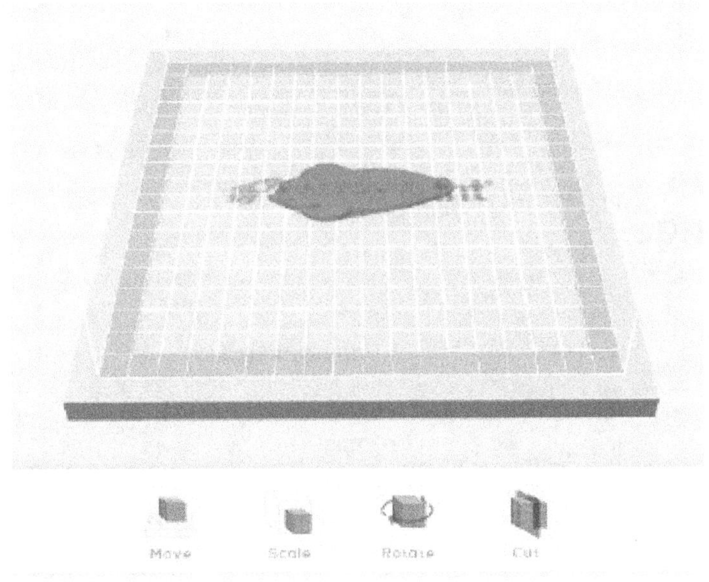

A slicer is a software that prepares a 3d model for printing. The process is calling slicing.

As part of the Ultimaker ecosystem, Cura was the most popular. Your 3d printer would come with a Cura based slicer software customized with a bunch of printer specific settings. **Ultimaker also has a free Cura edition available for download (Windows, Linux and Mac).**

Keep in mind, the one that comes with your printer may not be the latest version. If you upgrade to a new version, you must make sure the new version has all your printer specific settings.

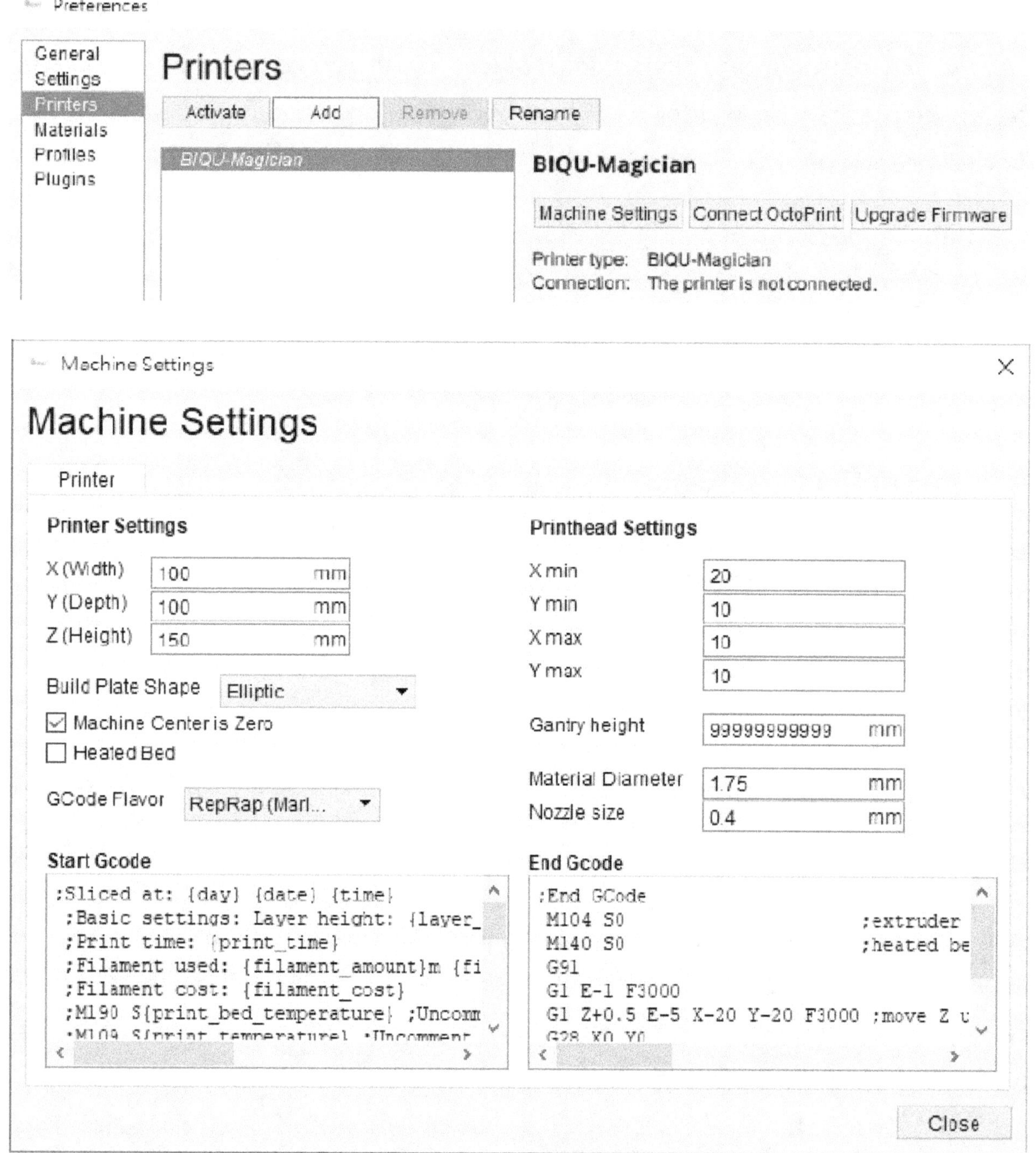

Machine settings and print quality expectations together would form a print profile for keeping 3d printer related settings on print quality. It is printer specific (that's why the slicer software that comes with your printer would have this profile already included). If you are using a non-supported platform, you may need to configure the profile manually (the machine setting must be correct).

A proper profile should include information on the bed size/shape and shape as well as the number of extruder and the nozzle diameter (there is a small marking on the nozzle stating the diameter.)...etc.

The bed shape and size is directly related to the size of object your printer can print.

The bed is either rectangular or circular. Cartesian printers always have rectangular bed. Delta printers, in contrast, always use circular bed. You must pick the correct one in order to print properly.

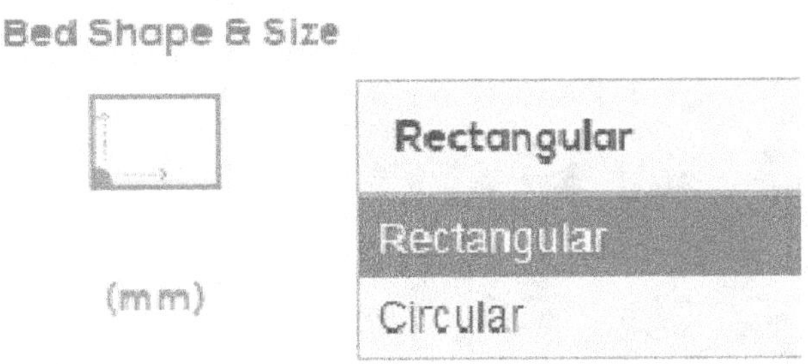

When the object is not properly "placed" on the bed, the slicer will have nothing to slice. You can move the object manually to make sure it sits on the bed.

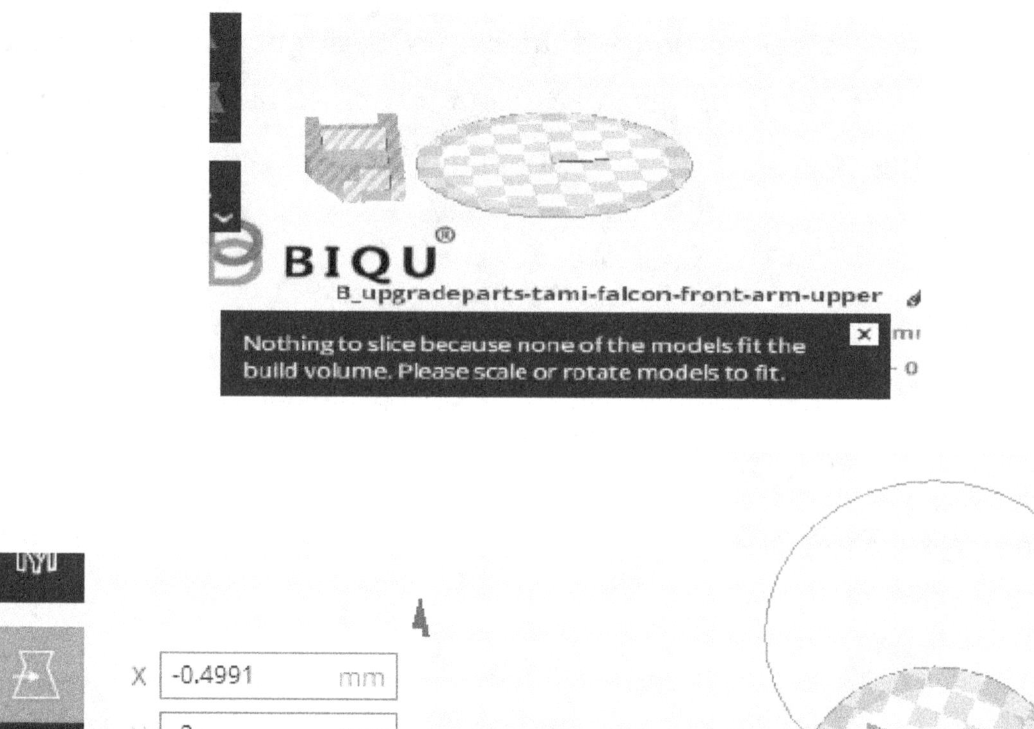

If you do not have Cura, there are other free alternatives. For example: Slic3r is open source and free. Craftware is another.

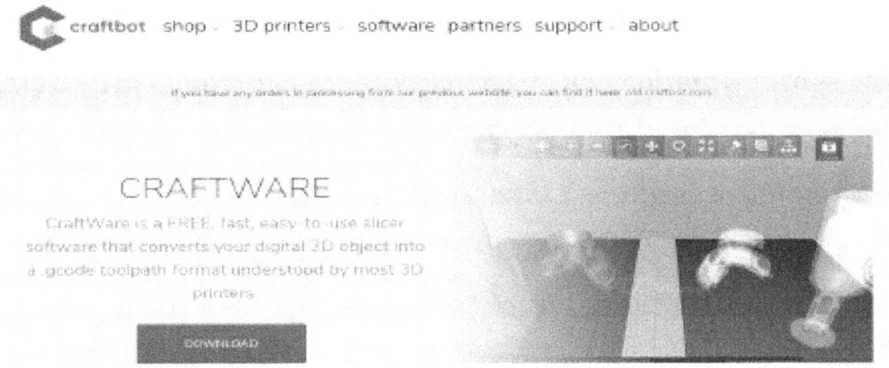

There are also cloud based slicers, such as Astroprint. If your internet connection is fast and stable, this would be a pretty nice option.

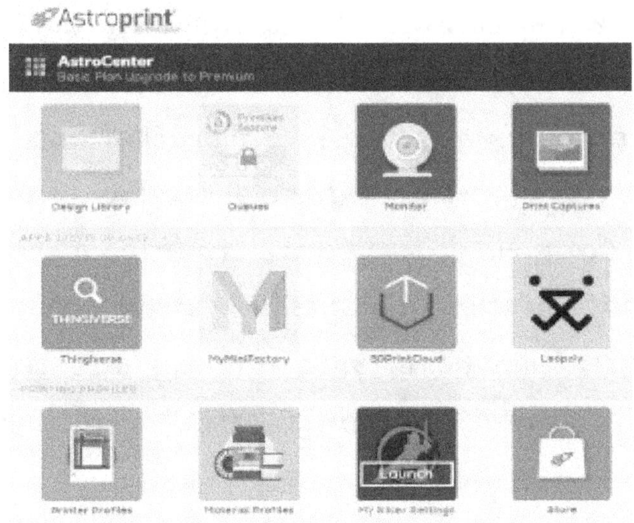

Do note that the Cura engine is always working behind the scene (it serves as the backend slicing engine of many cloud based slicers).

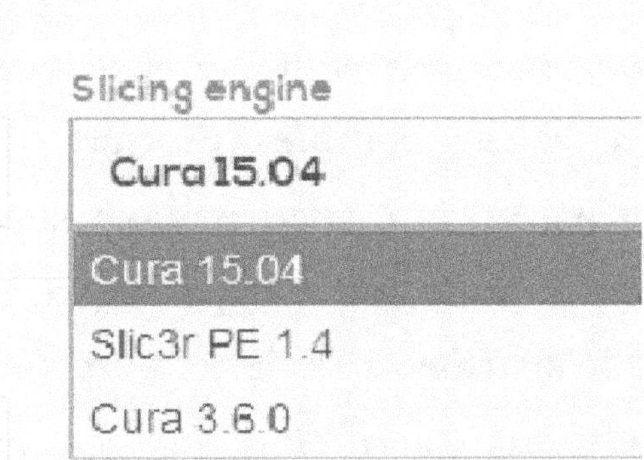

While Cura is often cited as the most widely used slicer overall, it is not definitively the most popular or best choice specifically for Delta printers in 2026. The landscape has shifted considerably, and newer alternatives like OrcaSlicer have gained significant traction, particularly among users who want advanced features and calibration tools optimized for various printer kinematics, including Deltas. To understand which slicer truly dominates for Delta printers, one must consider the strengths and weaknesses of the leading options.

Cura remains a safe and accessible starting point for many Delta owners, especially beginners. Its primary advantage is the massive library of pre-configured profiles for many common Delta models, such as those from FLSUN. This means a new user can often download Cura, select their printer from a list, and start printing with minimal setup or calibration hassle. The enormous user base also means a wealth of online tutorials, plugins, and community support specifically tailored to Cura. However, Cura's traditional strength has not been in high-speed printing optimization, and its advanced calibration tools rely on a plugin ecosystem rather than being built directly into the software. For users wanting to push a Delta printer to its limits, this can feel like an extra hurdle.

The strongest challenger to Cura's popularity among experienced Delta users is OrcaSlicer. This slicer has emerged as a top recommendation specifically because it addresses the two biggest challenges of Delta printing, calibration and speed optimization, directly within the application. Delta printers are known for being sensitive to calibration, and OrcaSlicer's integrated wizards for temperature, flow rate, and pressure advance are major time savers that can dramatically improve print quality on a Delta's complex motion system. Additionally, Deltas are capable of very fast printing, but they need a slicer that can keep up with their kinematics. OrcaSlicer is built with high-speed printing in mind, offering fine-tuned controls for acceleration and jerk that help users push their Delta printers to their limits without sacrificing surface quality. As a community-driven fork of Bambu Studio, OrcaSlicer is under rapid development, constantly integrating the best features from across the open-source ecosystem. For intermediate and advanced users who are not getting the speed or surface finish they want from Cura, OrcaSlicer has become a favorite.

PrusaSlicer occupies a middle ground. It is highly respected for its accuracy and clean G-code generation, and it works well with most FDM printers including Deltas, though it offers fewer pre-configured Delta profiles than Cura. Its interface appeals to methodical users who prioritize dimensional accuracy and manual control over every parameter. However, it lacks the built-in high-speed calibration tools of OrcaSlicer and does not have the massive pre-configured profile library of Cura, so it tends to be chosen by users who are already familiar with the Prusa ecosystem rather than those specifically seeking a Delta-optimized slicer.

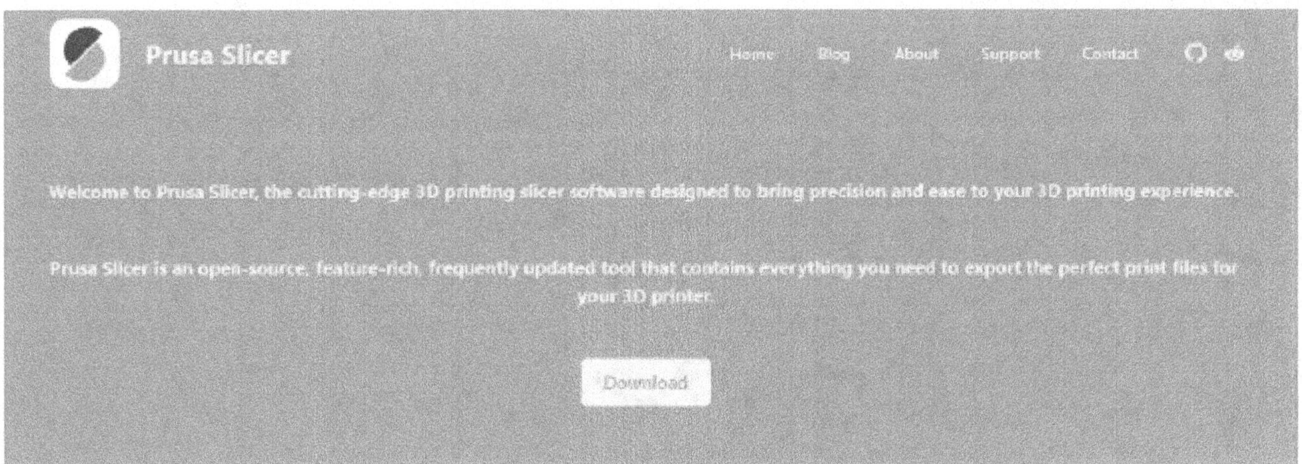

Prusa Slicer, developed by Prusa Research, is a highly versatile and open-source slicing software designed for 3D printing enthusiasts and professionals. It has gained widespread popularity due to its robust feature set, adaptability, and strong community support. This tool, based on the Slic3r software, has evolved significantly, incorporating advanced features that cater to a broad spectrum of users, from beginners to experts.

3D Printers & Scanners

Preparing the model

In the world of 3d modeling and printing, the Export function is used for converting your creation into mesh based file that can be further processed for 3d printing. The most popular mesh based file format for 3d printing is STL. In Windows 10 the 3D viewer feature can open and view STL files.

To print a model, first of all you must export your 3d model to STL. Then you open up the STL file from the slicer. The slicer takes the STL file and prepare a special Gcode file that can be printed.

The first section of the file contains a bunch of instructions.

```
1    ;FLAVOR:RepRap
2    ;TIME:1232
3    ;Filament used: 2.69509m
4    ;Layer height: 0.4
5    ;Generated with Cura_SteamEngine 0.0.0-master
6    M104 S200
7    M109 S200
8    ;Sliced at: Tue 01-09-2020 22:04:45
9    ;Basic settings: Layer height: 0.4 Walls: 1.2 Fill: {fill_density}
10   ;Print time: 00:20:33
11   ;Filament used: [2.7]m [8.038241874999999]g
12   ;Filament cost: [0]
13   ;M190 S60 ;Uncomment to add your own bed temperature line
14   ;M109 S200 ;Uncomment to add your own temperature line
15   G21            ;metric values
16   G90            ;absolute positioning
17   M82            ;set extruder to absolute mode
18   M107           ;start with the fan off
19   G28 X0 Y0   ;move X/Y to min endstops
20   G28 Z0      ;move Z to min endstops
21   G1 Z15.0 F3000 ;move the platform down 15mm
22   G92 E0                  ;zero the extruded length
23   G1 F3000 E3              ;extrude 3mm of feed stock
24   G92 E0                  ;zero the extruded length again
25   G1 F3000
26   ;Put printing message on LCD screen
27   M117 Printing...
28   ;LAYER_COUNT:48
29   ;LAYER:0
30   M107
31   G0 F3600 X16.687 Y-5.049 Z0.3
```

The actual data section is like a map full of coordinates.

```
1287    G1 X12.45 Y21.658 E246.95822
1288    G1 X12.45 Y21.229 E246.96584
1289    G1 X12.45 Y20.89 E246.98344
1290    G1 X12.45 Y20.878 E246.98429
1291    G1 X12.45 Y-20.866 E249.76106
1292    G1 X12.45 Y-20.997 E249.76977
1293    G1 X12.45 Y-21.32 E249.75126
1294    G1 X12.449 Y-21.658 E249.81374
1295    G1 X12.634 Y-21.321
1296    G1 X12.796 Y-20.997 E249.82912
1297    G1 X12.847 Y-20.877 E249.83722
1298    G1 X12.972 Y-20.585 E249.85835
1299    G1 X13.056 Y-20.352 E249.87482
1300    G1 X13.136 Y-20.096 E249.89267
1301    G1 X13.203 Y-19.891 E249.9102
1302    G1 X13.263 Y-19.552 E249.92989
1303    G1 X13.304 Y-19.256 E249.94972
1304    G0 F7200 X13.321 Y-19.057
1305    G0 X12.996 Y-19.784
```

The Gcode file is in fact a text file which can be viewed with Notepad and the like. The file can be saved to a SD card directly through Cura (or you can manually copy the file to the SD card). Almost every 3D printer has a SD card slot for reading Gcode files. Some even allow you to connect directly to the computer via USB.

Between using an SD card and a direct USB connection from your computer, the SD card is widely considered the more reliable and safer choice for actual printing, especially for long or important jobs, while direct USB connection is generally better suited for short tests, printer tuning, and when using a dedicated host like a Raspberry Pi running OctoPrint.

The case for using an SD card rests primarily on stability and safety. For any print that will take more than an hour, the SD card method is strongly preferred by the community because it completely removes your computer from the equation. Your PC can go to sleep, update its software, or crash entirely, and your printer will continue its work uninterrupted since it is reading the G-code instructions directly from the card. This independence makes for a much safer setup, as a lost USB connection can leave your printer in a dangerous state where the nozzle and bed continue to heat while the movement stops, creating a potential fire hazard. The peace of mind that comes from knowing a long print will finish successfully regardless of what happens on your computer is something many users find easily outweighs the minor inconvenience of shuffling a small card from their computer to the printer. The only real downside to SD card printing is inconvenience, as it requires physically transferring files from your computer to the printer, which can feel cumbersome for frequent test prints.

The case for printing directly from a computer over USB is strongest during setup, calibration, and for very short prints. The ability to start a print directly from your slicer without saving a file to a card saves valuable time and effort when running quick test prints to calibrate your printer or fine-tune your slicer settings. When connected via USB, you also gain full control and monitoring capabilities, allowing you to watch temperatures in real time, manually move the print head, adjust feed rates, or cancel a job immediately if you see problems starting to form. However, this convenience comes with a significant risk. Any background process on your PC, from an automatic update to a software crash to simply putting the computer to sleep, can interrupt the data stream to the printer and ruin a job that might have taken hours to complete. For this reason, direct USB from a general-purpose computer is not recommended for long or important prints, as the risk of an interruption is simply too high.

There is a third option that offers the best of both worlds, using a dedicated host such as a Raspberry Pi running OctoPrint. This setup is distinct from plugging your printer directly into your main computer. A small, dedicated single-board computer runs a stable, lightweight operating system and is not used for other tasks like web browsing or gaming, so it is far less prone to the interruptions that make direct PC printing unreliable. With OctoPrint, you gain the convenience of a networked connection, allowing you to upload and start prints from a web browser on your PC, phone, or tablet, and even monitor the print with a live camera feed, all while maintaining the stability of an SD card style print because the dedicated host handles the G-code streaming reliably. Too complicated for beginners though.

FDM and "slices"

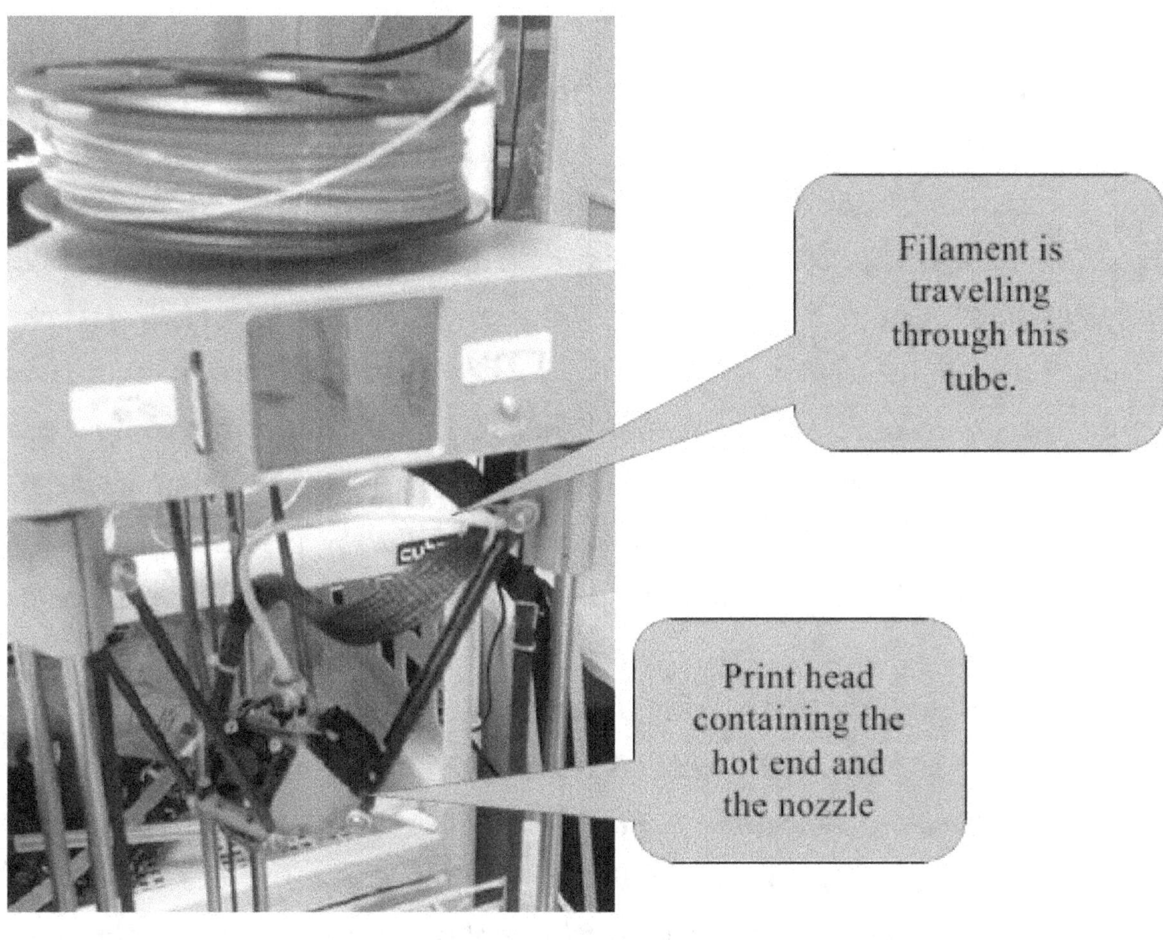

The term FDM stands for Fused Deposition Modeling, which is a trademarked name originally coined by Stratasys, though the more generic term is FFF or Fused Filament Fabrication. An FDM printer works by passing a plastic filament, which is essentially a long, thin string of thermoplastic material wound around a spool, along a PTFE tube or Bowden tube that guides it toward the hot end assembly. A motorized gear mechanism called the extruder, either pushing directly into the hot end in a direct drive configuration or pushing through a long tube in a Bowden configuration, squeezes the filament forward with considerable force. This force drives the filament into the hot end, where a heater cartridge raises the temperature high enough to melt the specific plastic being used, typically between one hundred eighty and two hundred sixty degrees Celsius depending on whether the material is PLA, ABS, PETG, or another thermoplastic.

As the filament melts due to the heat generated at the hot end, it transforms from a solid, rigid strand into a viscous, molten fluid that can flow under pressure. This pressurized molten plastic is forced through a small precision-machined opening at the tip of the hot end called the nozzle, which typically measures between 0.2 and 0.8 millimeters in diameter. The plastic exits the nozzle as a thin, continuous strand, almost like squeezing toothpaste from a tube or piping icing onto a cake. Once extruded, this strand is deposited in precise patterns onto the bed, which is also commonly referred to as the build plate or build surface. The bed is typically heated as well, especially for materials like ABS or PETG, to help the first layer stick and to prevent warping as the plastic cools.

The key to the entire process is thermal fusion. The layers are fused together because each new layer of extruded plastic is deposited while the layer beneath it is still hot enough to form a molecular bond. The molten plastic from the nozzle does not simply sit on top of the previous layer, it partially melts the surface of that previous layer upon contact, allowing the polymer chains from the two layers to entangle and fuse together as they cool. This is why the process is called fused deposition modeling, the deposition happens layer by layer, and the fusion happens because the material remains hot enough to weld itself to its predecessor. As the layers cool, they solidify and lock together, eventually forming a complete, solid three-dimensional object.

This brings us to why software like Cura, PrusaSlicer, and OrcaSlicer are called slicers. The term is wonderfully literal. A slicer takes a three-dimensional digital model, typically in a file format like STL, OBJ, or 3MF, and mathematically cuts it into hundreds or thousands of horizontal cross-sections. Each cross-section represents exactly one layer of the final printed object, with a thickness equal to the layer height setting chosen by the user, often between 0.1 and 0.3 millimeters. These slices are two-dimensional outlines that the printer can follow, much like a pen plotter drawing flat shapes one on top of another. The slicer then converts each of these two-dimensional slices into machine-readable G-code instructions that tell the printer exactly where to move the nozzle, how fast to move, how much filament to extrude, and when to raise the nozzle to begin the next layer. So when you load a model of a cube into Cura and click slice, the software is literally cutting that cube into, say, two hundred horizontal slices, each 0.2 millimeters thick, and then generating the toolpath that will create those slices one by one from molten plastic. The final object is essentially the accumulated stack of these slices, fused together so seamlessly that, when successful, you cannot even see the individual layers without close inspection.

FYI, the extruder is the bottleneck here. The reason is that the Delta motion system is so exceptionally fast and agile that it can easily outpace the relatively slow physical and thermal processes of melting and pushing plastic through a small nozzle. To understand this, consider first what each part of the printer does. The Delta motion system, with its lightweight arms and stationary motors, is designed for high speed and high acceleration. A well-tuned Delta can easily achieve travel speeds of three hundred to five hundred millimeters per second and accelerations of three thousand to ten thousand millimeters per second squared. The extruder, however, does not enjoy such liberating physics. The extruder's job is to take solid filament, melt it into a viscous fluid, and push that fluid through a tiny orifice typically 0.4 millimeters in diameter. This process is governed by thermal conductivity, viscosity, and pressure, none of which can be improved simply by moving the nozzle faster. The hot end can only transfer so much heat into the filament as it passes through. Every filament material has a maximum volumetric flow rate, measured in cubic millimeters per second, beyond which it simply cannot melt fast enough. For a standard brass nozzle and a typical hot end using PLA, that limit is often around ten to fifteen cubic millimeters per second. For a high-flow hot end with a longer melt zone and a stronger heater, that might reach thirty to fifty cubic millimeters per second. But even that is a hard ceiling.

Now let us do the math that reveals the bottleneck. The relationship between print speed and volumetric flow is straightforward. Volumetric flow rate in cubic millimeters per second equals print speed in millimeters per second multiplied by layer height in millimeters multiplied by extrusion width in millimeters. With a standard 0.4 millimeter nozzle, a reasonable layer height of 0.2 millimeters, and an extrusion width of 0.45 millimeters, the volumetric flow at one hundred millimeters per second is nine cubic millimeters per second, which is comfortably within the capability of a standard hot end. At two hundred millimeters per second, that same calculation yields eighteen cubic millimeters per second, which exceeds what a standard hot end can reliably melt. The Delta motion system would happily move the nozzle at two hundred millimeters per second or faster, but the plastic simply cannot be melted and pushed through the nozzle fast enough to keep up. The extruder becomes the bottleneck because the motion system is asking for more plastic than the hot end can supply.

This bottleneck manifests in several visible print defects. If the extruder cannot keep up with the requested flow, the nozzle will begin to under-extrude, creating gaps between lines, weak infill, and poor layer adhesion. The stepper motor driving the filament may begin to skip steps, producing a clicking sound as it fails to push the required amount of plastic. In severe cases, the filament can grind away against the drive gear, creating dust and losing grip entirely. Even if the hot end can technically melt the required volume, printing at the extreme limits of its flow rate often leads to printing at temperatures that are too high to maintain dimensional accuracy, oozing, and poor surface finish.

If the material feeding process isn't smooth or when the tube is loose, eventually you will find the remains of the PLA spilling all over the place where heat builds up:

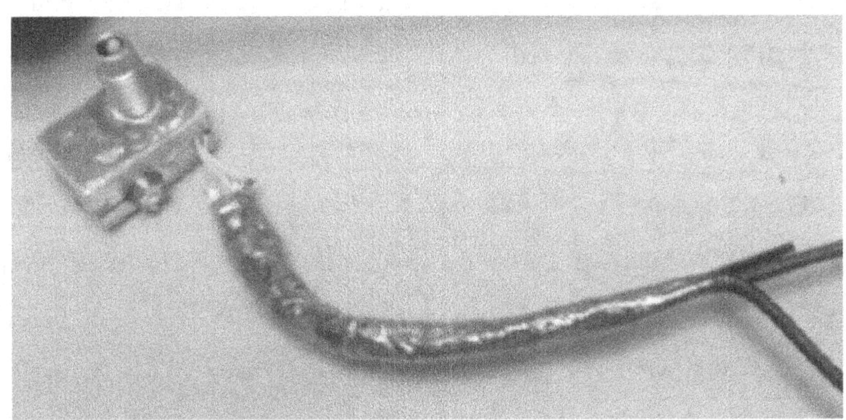

Poor material feeding can break the PLA inside the tube and lead to jamming. If the nozzle is too small the risk of jamming will increase as well. Larger nozzles (0.4mm or larger) are generally safer in this regard. 0.6mm or larger nozzle seldom jams.

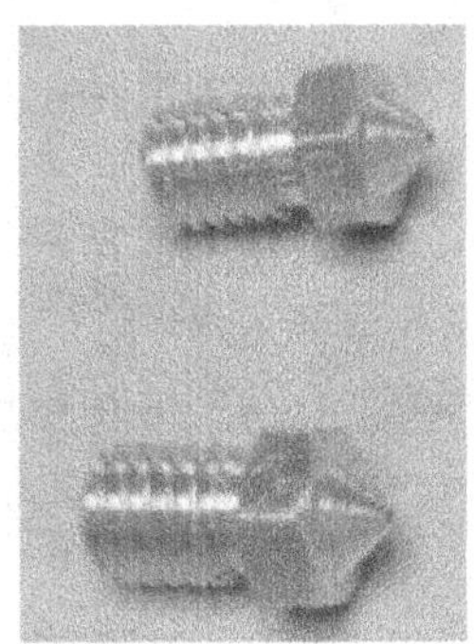

The brain of the printer

G-code is a special computer language. It tells the 3d printer how to print things. In particular it has commands carrying a bunch of assigned movement and action the 3d printer would follow.

As mentioned earlier, a 3d printer creates a 3D object by adding material on a layer-by-layer basis. Slicing is all about cutting a 3d object into horizontal 2d layers so that the object can be printed one slice at a time. It is like piling up a bunch of paper sheets each with different shapes so to form a 3d object.

The Gcode file has information on all the slices. The "brain" inside the 3D printer can interpret the information accordingly. Do note that some slicers also support the X3G format, which is less popular than Gcode.

There is a set of microcontroller and additional circuit boards /devices inside every printer. These electronic components together read the Gcode file and instruct the print head to print accordingly.

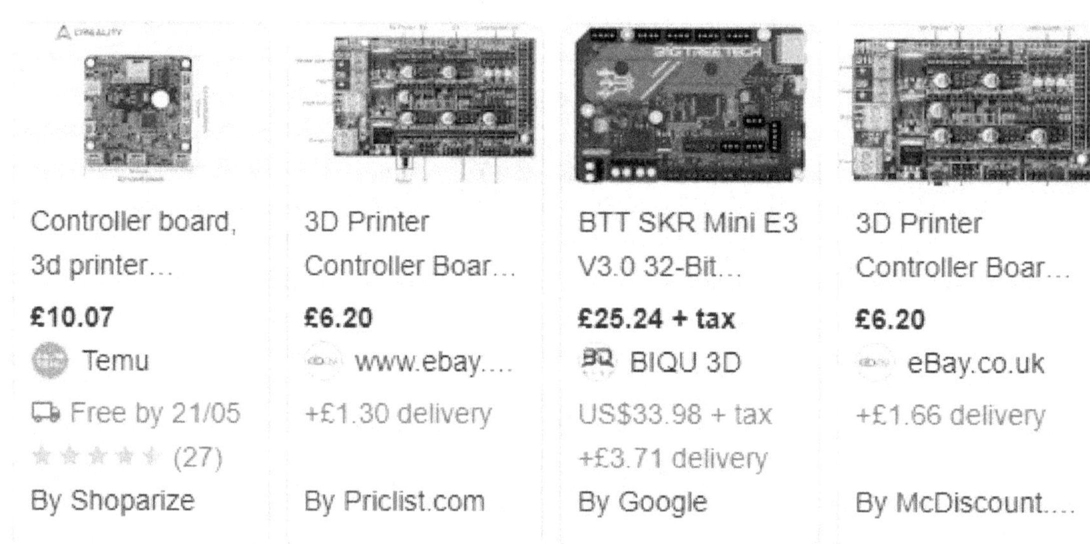

On a Delta printer, all the electronic stuff are housed at the top, with a cooling fan around for heat dissipation. They are pretty durable as long as the cooling fan doesn't stop working.

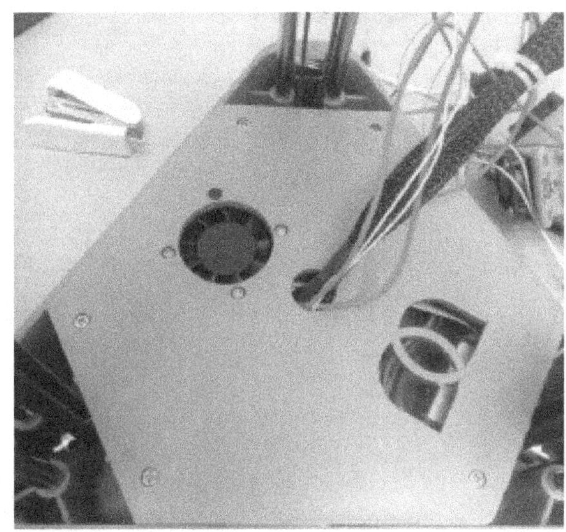

Aka MCU, a microcontroller is like a low cost simplified version of your regular computer, or some sort of system on a chip. Those found on a 3D printer are optimized for controlling the various parts so to 3d print your models.

The circuitry needs to offer high current capabilities as well as support for MOSFETs, movement systems, multiple extruders, LCD screen and printer firmware …etc. High current capabilities are particularly important as there is a need to heat up the hotend to up to 200 degrees or so! And there is also a connector for connecting to the thermistor for temperature detection. We will talk about the hotend in greater detail later in this book.

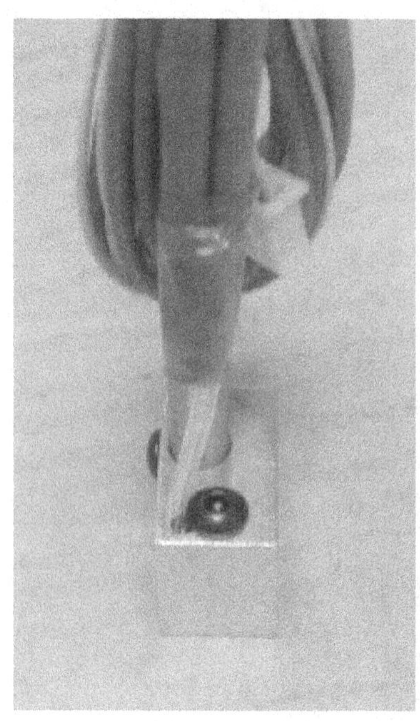

Older systems are 8 bit based. 32 bit boards are now very affordable! Some can provide power to the components directly, while some require help from special driver circuitry. If for whatever reason the circuitry is damaged, you should always replace the bad one with one of an exact same model.

Arduino seems to be quite popular these days. Different Arduino boards may be equipped with different chips, even though the Atmel (now owned by Microchip) controllers are the most popular ones. ATmega8, ATmega168, ATmega328, ATmega1280, and ATmega2560...etc. The primary difference that really has a meaning to a beginner is the amount of memory onboard. The Uno is the most popular one for starters. The Arduino Mega is like a more powerful version of the Uno.

The Arduino board alone does not offer 3d printing logic as it cannot talk to other components directly. There has to be a middleman in between. An example of such middleman is the RepRap Arduino Mega Polulu Shield RAMPS board, which has been widely deployed on the RepRap 3D printers.

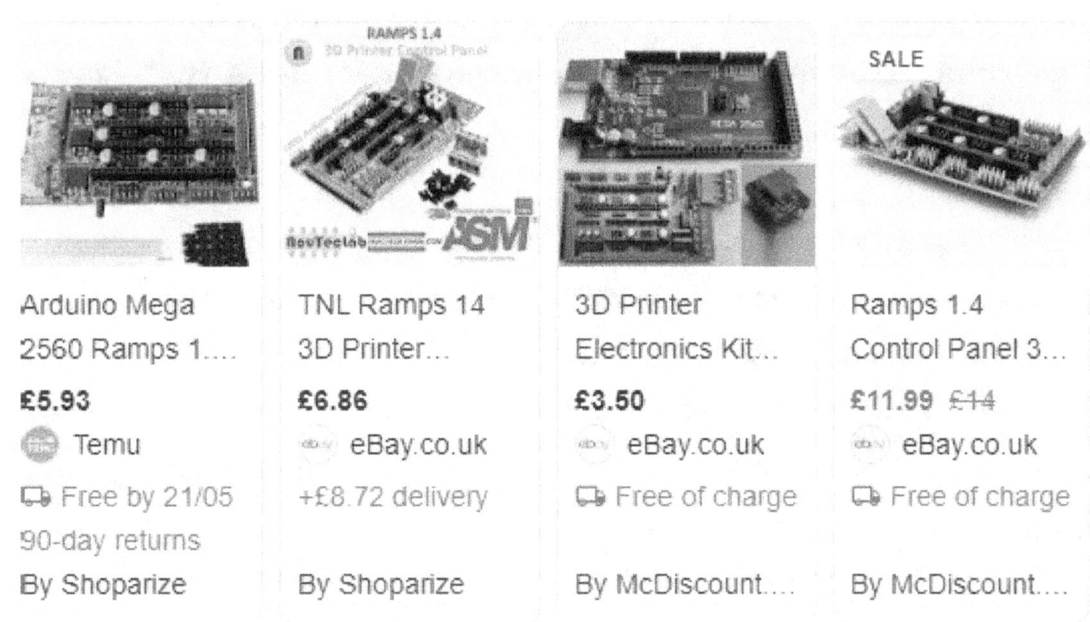

The compartment that houses the board is small so the power supply to the printer has to stay outside as a separate unit. There is a dedicated connector for it.

The reason most 3D printers use an external power supply comes down to a practical balance of safety, cost, heat management, and design simplicity. While a sleek, all-in-one machine with an internal power supply might seem ideal, the external power brick approach offers significant advantages that have made it the standard for consumer-grade printers.

The strongest argument for an external power supply is safety. Standard wall outlets provide high-voltage alternating current, but a printer's electronics, including its motors and control board, operate on low-voltage direct current. The power supply's job is to perform this critical conversion, and by keeping this high-energy conversion process outside the printer's main chassis, manufacturers create a physical barrier between the risky, high-voltage AC power and the rest of the printer. This is not a hypothetical concern, as there are well-documented cases of house fires caused by printer power supplies, particularly in cheaper models where low-quality internal components failed, leading to short circuits and overheating. Keeping the power supply external means the primary source of electrical risk is isolated, and in the event of a failure, it can be more easily and safely replaced without opening the printer's main case.

Closely related to safety is the challenge of heat management. The process of converting AC to DC generates a significant amount of heat, and an external power supply removes this heat source from the printer's enclosure. This is a major advantage because 3D printers are already sensitive to temperature fluctuations. Placing a hot power supply inside the printer could create uneven ambient temperatures, making it harder to control the print environment and potentially leading to warped or failed prints. The separate power brick can be placed away from the printer, where its own fan can cool it without interfering with the delicate thermal balance of the printing process.

Finally, the external approach offers flexibility, cost savings, and design simplicity. A printer's power supply is a standardized, off-the-shelf component, and by keeping it external, manufacturers can avoid the complex and costly engineering of integrating it into a single custom-molded case. For the user, this modularity is also a benefit. If a power supply fails, you do not need to send your entire printer in for repair, you can simply disconnect the old brick and plug in a new, widely available replacement. This also lowers the barrier for hobbyists who want to upgrade to a more powerful or quieter power supply, as it becomes a simple swap rather than a major rewiring project.

The alternative of an internal power supply is not without its merits, which is why some higher-end or more integrated machines use it. The main advantage is a clean, compact, and professional appearance. By integrating the power supply into the printer's base or frame, manufacturers can create a single, self-contained unit without an external brick and its trailing wires, a design often preferred for offices or homes where aesthetics are a priority. However, this sleekness comes with significant trade-offs. An internal supply requires more complex engineering for safety and cooling, necessitating premium components that can handle the heat and often requiring a larger, more robust printer frame to safely house the electronics. These design challenges increase the manufacturer's costs, which are ultimately passed on to the consumer. As a result, printers with internal power supplies are generally more expensive, professional-grade machines that have the budget and design space to overcome these engineering hurdles.

For the vast majority of consumer 3D printers, therefore, the external power supply is the superior choice because it prioritizes safety and reliability, which are far more critical for a successful print than a slightly cleaner desk setup.

RUZIZAO DC
Power Supply...
£39.96 & more prices
a Amazon.c... & more
Free delivery
5.0 ★★★★★ (2)

Creality 3D PSU
CM-350-24V, 3D...
£37.50 & more prices
3djake.uk & more
4.4 ★★★★★ (15)

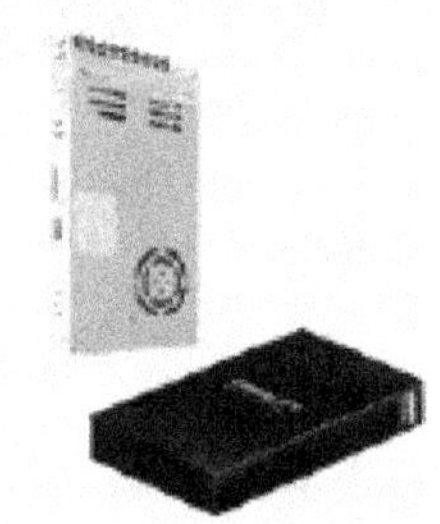

Creality Ender-3 V3
SE/KE 350W Power
Supply, Safe and...
£50.72
a Amazon.co.uk
Free delivery

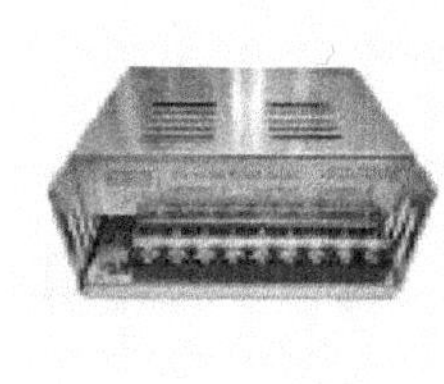

12v & 24v 3D
Printer Power
Supply - 15A, 20A...
£27.50
eBay
Free delivery

Velleman 3D Printer
Power Supply Unit
£23.27
Velleman
Free delivery on £50+

The material

Shorts for Polylactic Acid, PLA is by far the most popular materials used for small scale 3D printing. True PLA is mostly biodegradable. It comes in different colors, different weights and different sizes.

Entry level PLA is usually 1.75mm (the next step up is 3mm) and is requiring an extruder temperature approximately at or over 200 degree celsius.

Name

PLA

Filament Diameter

1.75 mm

Filament Density

PLA - 1.25 g/cm3

Extruder Temperature

220   °C

There are many different PLA suppliers out there. Generally speaking, the temperature rating for a particular PLA should be similar as long as they come from the same supplier.

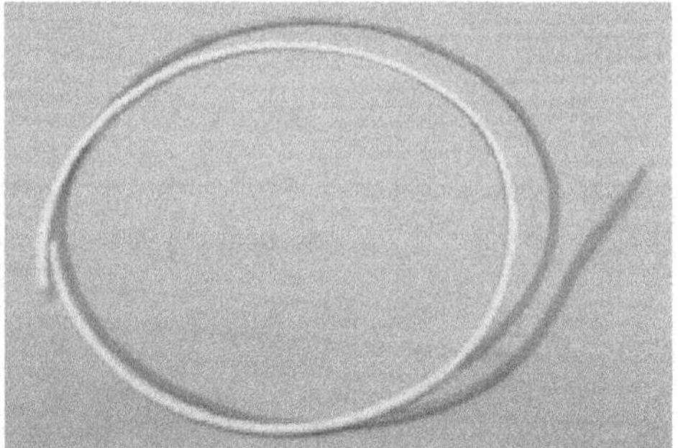

In reality, there may be small differences in the optimal temperature for PLA of different colors (in particular, clear PLA vs colored PLA), even though the differences may not always be significant.

PLA works anywhere from 180 to 230°C, although it is widely believed that 210°C is the best.

Generally, when you print a file, the printer will automatically adjust the temperature and heat things up. Still there is usually a function that allows you to manually heat up the PLA.

ABS requires a higher temperature (250°C) as well as a heated bed. It also generates smell which is no good in a typical indoor environment without very good ventilation.

Poor quality PLA tend to break easily which may get stuck somewhere inside the tube or at the hotend/nozzle:

The plastic tube where the material passes through does not require replacement UNLESS a small fragment of the PLA gets stuck in the middle and there is no way to take it out ....

Improper storage can also weaken the material. Filaments absorb moisture and weaken themselves over time. When there is severe stringing, cracking, or oozing, chance is that the filament is too wet to be used.

If you want to keep and use them, the safe and easy way is to place them right next to a dehumidifier for several cycles. Putting them in a food dehydrator with a temperature of around 40°C for PLA may also do the magic. There are other dedicated drying devices that are too costly for starters.

Before committing to printing something large, always check and make sure the material is not getting stuck somewhere in the spool! See this photo:

Feeding is technically jammed. If you discover this when printing is half way done, press the PAUSE button of the printer to put the process on hold, then take out the material and solve the problem before putting it back in to the feeder. RESUME printing asap and avoid unnecessary delay.

When we talk about 1.75mm filament, we are referring to the diameter of the plastic strand that feeds into your 3D printer. The filament is a long, thin, spaghetti like thread of plastic that is wound around a spool. That thread has a circular cross section, and the distance straight through the center of that circle from one edge to the opposite edge is the diameter. So 1.75mm filament is a plastic thread that measures 1.75 millimeters across. To give you a sense of scale, a standard paperclip is about one millimeter thick, so 1.75mm is a bit thicker than a paperclip but still quite thin. The alternative standard, which is much less common today, is 2.85mm filament, sometimes still called 3mm filament, which is almost twice as thick. Your printer is designed to accept filament of a specific diameter, and using the wrong diameter will cause severe under extrusion or over extrusion because the printer's calculations for how much plastic is being pushed through the nozzle will be completely wrong.

Now let me explain why 1.75mm became the dominant standard. The story goes back to the earliest days of desktop 3D printing around 2009. The very first hobbyist printers did not have a dedicated filament industry to supply them. The early pioneers, including the inventors of the RepRap project, had to find a readily available source of plastic strand. They discovered that plastic welding rod, which is used with hand held plastic welders to repair things like car bumpers and kayaks, was available in a diameter of approximately 3 millimeters. So the earliest 3D printers were designed to use that 3mm welding rod. This was a clever solution because it made the first printers possible without waiting for a new industry to emerge.

However, that 3mm filament had a serious problem. It was stiff and brittle. Imagine trying to bend a thick plastic rod. It resists bending, and if you force it too far, it will snap rather than bend gracefully. This brittleness became a major issue as users ran their printers. When the spool of 3mm filament was nearly empty and the plastic had to be pulled from the outer edge of the spool at a sharp angle, the stress of being forced out of its natural coiled shape would often cause the filament to snap. A snapped filament means your printer stops feeding plastic in the middle of a print, which ruins the print. Because the filament was thick and stiff, it also required a very strong extruder motor to push it through the hot end, and it was harder to control for fine detail work.

The shift toward thinner filament started when manufacturers realized that a smaller diameter could solve the brittleness problem. A 1.75mm filament is much more flexible than a 3mm filament. Think of the difference between a thick plastic coat hanger and a thin plastic zip tie. The thick one snaps when you bend it too far, but the thin one bends and flexes without breaking. That flexibility means 1.75mm filament can be pulled from a spool at sharp angles, guided through tight curves in a Bowden tube, and fed into the extruder without snapping. This made printers far more reliable. You could start a long print and walk away without worrying that the filament would snap near the end of the spool and ruin everything.

The flexibility of 1.75mm also enabled the use of Bowden extruders, where the extruder motor is mounted on the printer's frame rather than directly on the print head. In a Bowden setup, the filament is pushed through a long, flexible PTFE tube from the frame all the way to the hot end. This design makes the print head much lighter because the heavy extruder motor is not moving around, which allows for faster printing speeds and less shaking. However, Bowden systems only work well if the filament is flexible enough to navigate the tube without excessive friction. The stiff 3mm filament was poorly suited for Bowden setups, while 1.75mm filament worked beautifully.

Another advantage of 1.75mm filament is that it melts more quickly and consistently inside the hot end. Because the strand is thinner, the heat from the nozzle can penetrate to the center of the filament faster, ensuring that the plastic is fully molten before it is extruded. This allows for higher print speeds and better flow control. A thicker 2.85mm filament has a larger core that takes longer to reach the correct temperature, which can lead to inconsistent extrusion if you try to print too fast.

The industry rapidly converged on 1.75mm as the standard. Today, well over eighty percent of desktop 3D printers are designed for 1.75mm filament. This widespread adoption has created a virtuous cycle. Because so many printers use 1.75mm, filament manufacturers produce a huge variety of materials in that diameter, including PLA, PETG, ABS, TPU, nylon, polycarbonate, and all sorts of specialty composites like wood fill, carbon fiber, and glow in the dark. The competition among manufacturers keeps prices low, and you can buy a kilogram spool of standard PLA for around twenty dollars. Conversely, 2.85mm filament is now a niche product. It is still available, and some excellent printers like certain Ultimaker and LulzBot models still use it, but your selection of colors and materials is much more limited, and prices are often higher.

The 2.85mm filament, sometimes still called 3mm, has not completely disappeared. Some industrial and high end printers prefer the thicker diameter because it can be extruded at very high volumetric flow rates for large prints. The stiffness of 2.85mm can also be an advantage in very long Bowden tubes because it does not buckle as easily when pushed over long distances. However, for the overwhelming majority of home users, schools, and small businesses, 1.75mm filament is the standard, and it is what you will find on the shelves of any store that sells 3D printing supplies.

Apart from PLA, Delta printers can handle a remarkably wide range of materials, from common engineering plastics to flexible filaments and even exotic pastes like clay or chocolate. The key is that a Delta printer's capability depends more on its specific hardware features, such as the extruder type and maximum hotend temperature, rather than on its delta kinematics alone. Understanding which materials work well requires looking at both the inherent advantages of the Delta design and the necessary upgrades for more demanding filaments.

For standard and engineering materials, most Delta printers handle common filaments like ABS, PETG, and ASA without significant modification. These materials offer better heat resistance and durability than PLA. However, materials like ABS, ASA, nylon, and polycarbonate typically require a heated bed and, more importantly, an enclosed build chamber to prevent warping. The Delta design actually accommodates this well because the stationary bed and vertically oriented arms mean that adding an enclosure is straightforward, and the electronics can often be placed outside the hot enclosure for protection. Without an enclosure, these materials are prone to curling and layer separation due to uneven cooling.

For flexible filaments such as TPU and other thermoplastic elastomers, the Delta printer's stationary print bed offers a distinct advantage. Because the bed does not move back and forth during printing, the flexible part being printed remains still and does not wobble or get knocked over by the nozzle, which is a common problem on Cartesian bedslinger designs where the heavy bed shifts direction constantly. However, there is a critical hardware requirement for printing flexible materials on a Delta. The printer absolutely needs a direct drive extruder, where the motor sits directly above the hotend and pushes filament through a very short path. A Bowden extruder, where the motor is mounted on the frame and pushes filament through a long tube, will almost certainly cause the soft TPU to buckle, compress, and jam inside the tube, leading to failed prints. Many Delta printers come with Bowden setups by default, so printing flexible filaments often requires a conversion to direct drive or selecting a Delta model specifically designed for it.

For abrasive or filled materials, such as carbon fiber reinforced nylon, glass fiber composites, or filaments containing wood or metal particles, the primary concern is not the printer's motion system but the nozzle. These abrasive particles will quickly erode a standard brass nozzle, enlarging the orifice and ruining print precision, often within a few hours of printing. A hardened steel nozzle is required to resist this wear and maintain consistent extrusion. Additionally, using a larger diameter nozzle, 0.6 millimeters or larger, helps prevent clogs because the abrasive particles can pass through more easily than through a tiny 0.4 millimeter opening. The Delta printer itself handles these materials well, as the lightweight effector reduces vibration that could otherwise cause surface defects, but the nozzle upgrade is non-negotiable.

Temperature control

Cooling fans are necessary in two locations: the compartment that houses all the electronics, and the print head. On most Delta printer head, there are 3cm x 3cm fans "surrounding" the structure. Some are 5V while some are 12V.

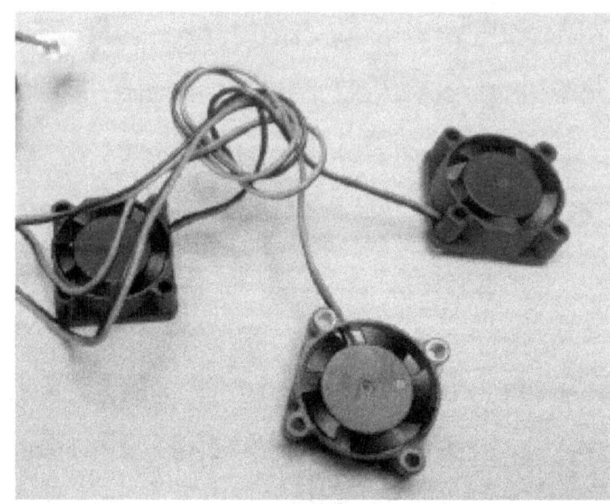

PLA works best with the cooling fan on (nylon, in contrast, should avoid cooling fan altogether). Most entry level printers assume that you are using PLA so the fan settings are already correct. You may, on some printers, manually turn on and off fans as needed.

Generally there is no need to change any of the fan speed settings.

FAN SETTINGS

Enable Fan
☑

Minimum Fan Speed

%

Maximum Fan Speed

%

Fan Full Height

mm

When the temperature of the hot end is too high, string and oozing can occur. Stringing refers to hairy prints that take place when small strings of plastic are left behind when oozing out of the nozzle while the print head is already moving to somewhere else. Improper temperature can cause this to happen. Try to lower the extruder temperature by a little bit (say, 10 degrees or so) and see how things go.

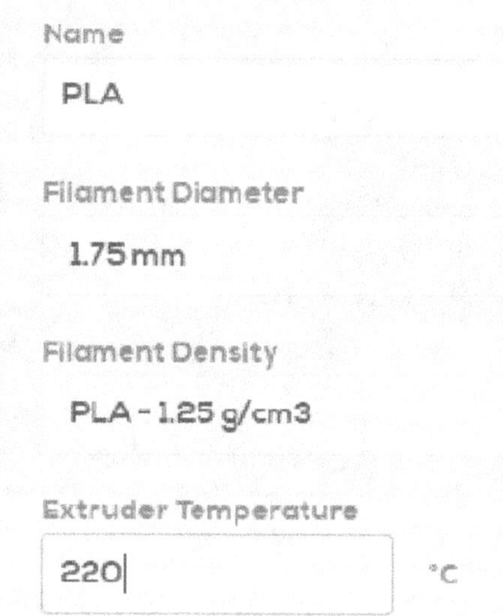

Always check and make sure all wires towards the hotend heater block are intact. There are two sets of wires to the heater block. The first set has 2 wires of the same color. They carry high current for heating things up. They are VERY EASY to break. If they really break, the print head will never get heated up.

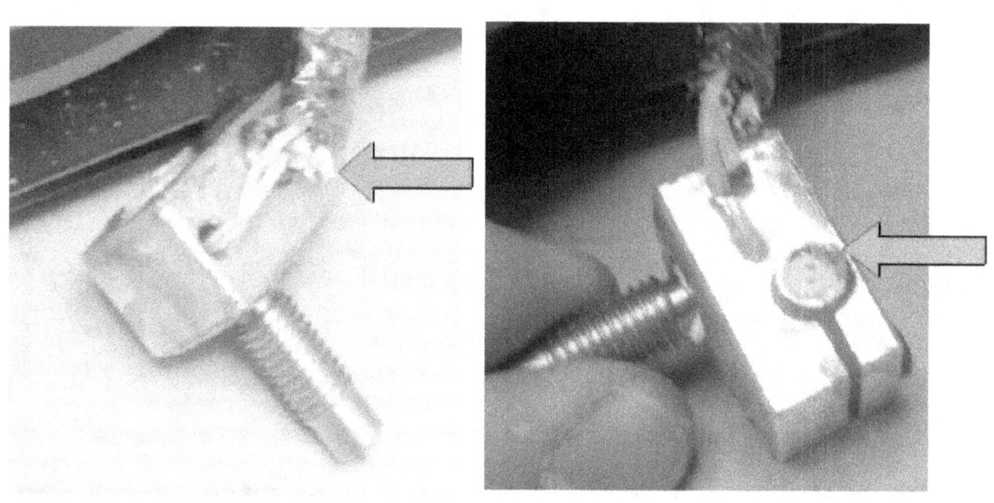

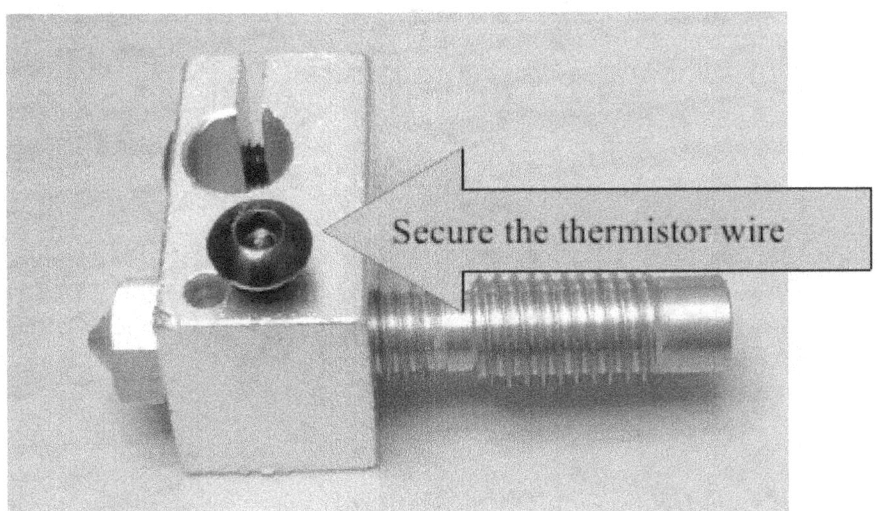

Another set of wires have a transparent look and are for the thermistor (a resistor whose resistance is temperature dependent). If it is loose, temperature detection becomes inaccurate and problem will occur.

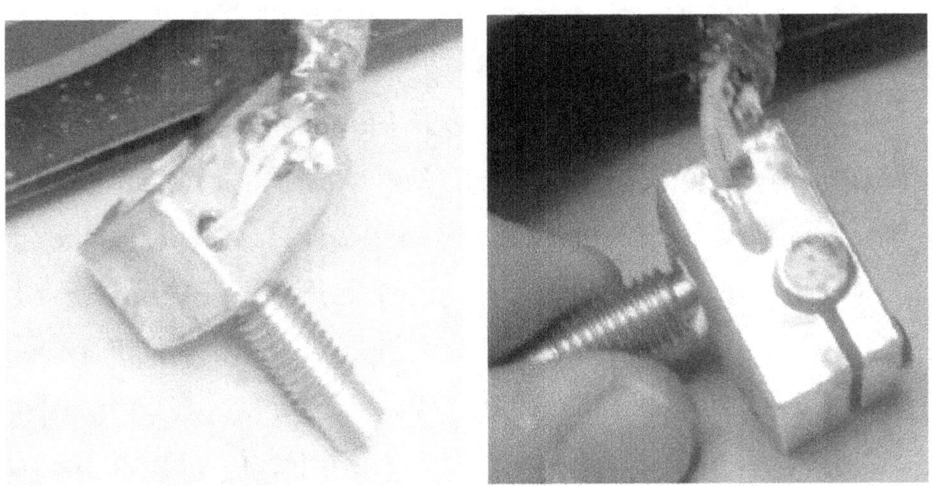

FYI, the cooling fans do not require special maintenance. There is no need to lube them. All you need is to keep them clean and dust free.

Setting the cooling fan correctly for a Delta printer is less about its unique delta geometry and more about following the same principles that apply to all FDM printers. The core rule is simple: different materials have different cooling needs. The challenge is that on many Delta printers, the cooling fan design can be a weak point, which makes proper settings more critical. The layer fan, which is the part-cooling fan and not the fan attached to the hotend's heatsink, must be adjusted according to the material being printed.

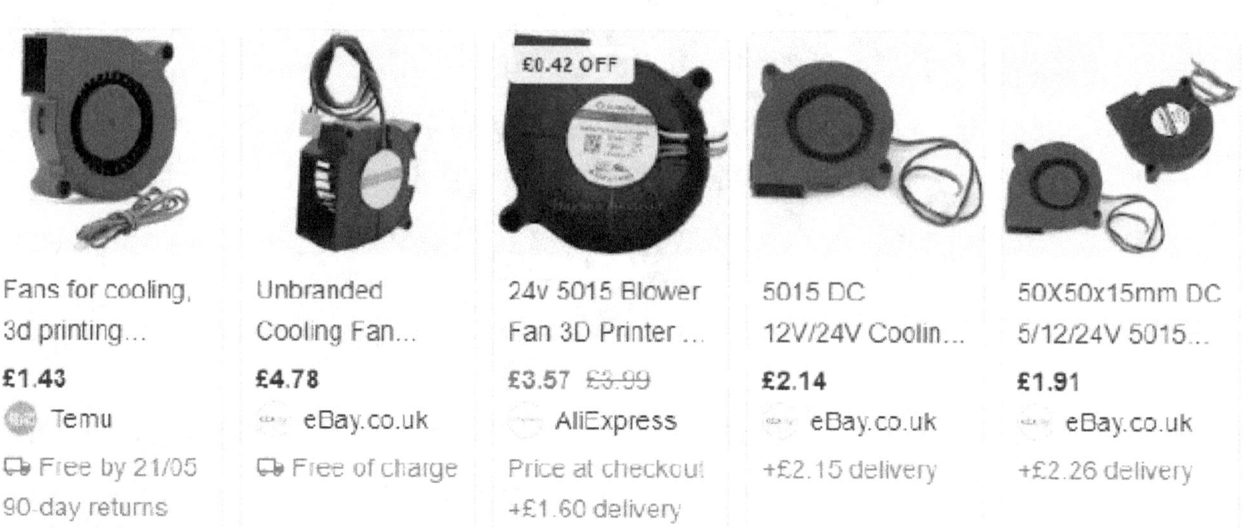

For PLA, the fan should be set to one hundred percent after the first few layers. PLA needs maximum cooling to solidify quickly for good detail and sharp overhangs, though the fan should remain off for the first one to three layers to help the bottom stick to the bed. For PETG, a much lower fan speed between twenty and sixty percent is appropriate, because too much cooling causes poor layer adhesion and a dull, matte finish. Good bridging may still require higher speeds up to one hundred percent, but this should be used conservatively. For ABS and ASA, the fan should be turned off completely. These materials are highly sensitive to cooling, and any fan use will cause layers to separate, curl, and warp. They require a warm, enclosed environment instead of active part cooling.

For flexible TPU, it is best to start with the fan off, and if cooling is needed for bridging or fine details, a very low setting up to fifty percent is acceptable, as cooling can prevent the flexible layers from bonding well to each other. For bridges and overhangs on all materials except ABS and ASA, increasing the fan temporarily to one hundred percent while the printer spans a gap or prints a steep overhang will improve results, after which the fan should return to its base speed.

While these speed percentages are universal, Delta printers have a unique quirk because many use a fan and duct setup that only cools the print from one side. Because Delta printers move fast and often have round, tower-like frames, a single fan can lead to the good side, bad side effect, where overhangs look great on one side but droop on the other.

There are several remedies for this issue. The best solution is to print a dual-fan duct upgrade, as many Delta owners upgrade to a custom duct that directs air from two opposite sides, providing even cooling all around. If that is not possible, orienting the part wisely on the build plate by rotating the model so the most challenging overhang or detailed area faces the cooling fan directly will help. Additionally, printing slower for delicate features gives a single fan enough time to cool the plastic before the next layer goes down.

Beyond these material-specific rules, several advanced slicer settings can dramatically improve results regardless of printer type. Disabling the fan for the first layers gives the bottom of the print time to grip the bed without being cooled and popping off. Using dynamic fan speeds for overhangs and bridges allows the slicer to intelligently manage fan speed, running at a low percentage for normal printing but automatically jumping to one hundred percent when it detects a bridge or a severe overhang, which prevents the sagging that happens when hot plastic has nothing beneath it.

Setting a minimum layer time is also important, because if a layer is very small, such as the tip of a spire, the printer will finish it in seconds, leaving the plastic molten. The minimum layer time setting forces the printer to either slow down or wait a few seconds, giving the part cooling fan time to solidify the plastic before the next layer is added. Finally, the heatsink fan that points directly at the hotend's cooling block should never be disabled. If that fan is not running, the filament will melt too high up, causing a jam, so this fan should be set to one hundred percent at all times.

To find the perfect setting for a specific filament, the tuning process is the same for a Delta as any other printer. Printing a calibration test such as an overhang test or a temperature tower that includes bridging sections will provide clear data. Observing the results closely to find where overhangs look the cleanest and most defined without showing signs of curling or drooping will reveal the optimal speed. Adjusting the slicer settings once that speed is found establishes the default maximum fan speed for that specific material. The ideal setting is always a balance, enough cooling to manage overhangs and details, but not so much that it weakens the bonds between the layers. Understanding this trade-off is the key to mastering any Delta printer.

Layer height and thickness

Layer height is a parameter directly related to how smooth and detailed the printout can get. An object printed with thinner layers will have a smoother surface and can produce finer details. Some entry level slicer software has this setting tied to a quality profile so you do not need to manually specify the layer height.

Generally, a print quality of 0.1mm or so is considered as fine while 0.2mm is average. Anything over 0.3mm can have a rough look.

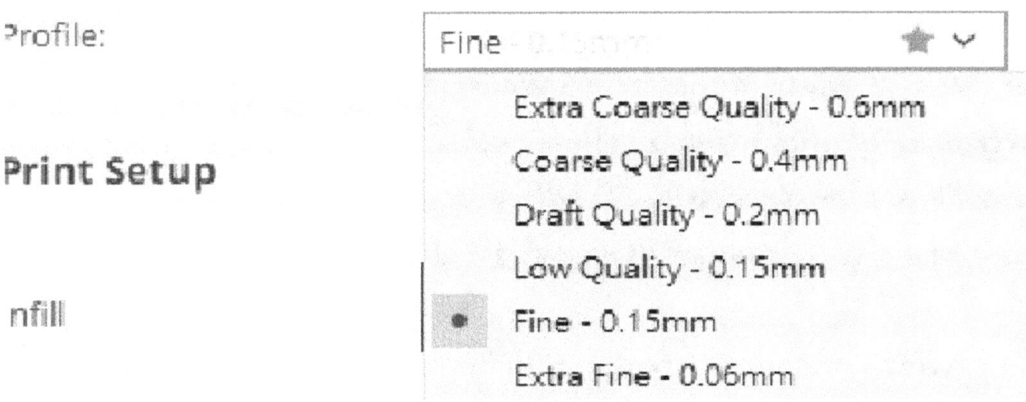

HOWEVER, a layer height too fine may introduce difficulty in plate adhesion (what is extruded simply doesn't stick to the bed). Experience shows that anything under 0.4mm may require the use of stronger glue on the print bed for proper plate adhesion to occur!

Even if you have the proper layer height, the smaller the object to print the harder it will be for adhesion to take place. If you are printing something with a diameter of 6mm or so (such as a plastic bushing), chance is that you will have almost no adhesion at all...

Nozzle diameter is a physical property of the nozzle, which is not the same as the print quality or layer height. 0.3 and 0.4mm nozzles are pretty common.

The tricky part is on choosing a layer height that works best with the physical nozzle size while achieving a proper balance between surface smoothness and strength as well as plate adhesion. Always remember, plate adhesion is about how the extruded filament can properly stick to the bed without moving away. Your print will not be successful if adhesion is poor. Imagine what is going to happen if the print warps when it is about half way completed...

A higher line width means a stronger print. A nozzle with a greater diameter can provide a higher line width and therefore more strength. The smaller the nozzle diameter, the higher detail you can print at the expense of printing time (it takes longer time to extrude sufficient filament) and the risk of clogging (anything less than 0.3mm can be very easy to clog). If you use a nozzle with a large diameter, it can produce stronger print at higher speed while consuming filament much faster.

Expecting 0.1mm extra fine output with a 0.4mm nozzle does not make sense. On the other hand, expecting 0.4mm output with a 0.2mm nozzle may be too inefficient. Some careful testing and trials would be necessary to find out the best possible balance.

Changing the nozzle is nothing difficult. All you need is a hex wrench capable of handling M4 nuts.

You need to use a clamp to hold the hotend block tight while unscrewing the nozzle. When putting in a new nozzle, wrap a thin layer of water pipe seal tape around the thread to prevent leaking. (leaking of molten material can occur).

Some software even allow you to perform more quality related settings. For example, with Astroprint you can specify the layer height of the first layer that sits on the bed.

Some suggest that the max layer height should be around 50% the physical width of the nozzle.

First layer height is special as it is directly related to plate adhesion:

It is always recommended that you have the first layer (the layer that sits on the bed) printed with double thickness so that the first layer can absorb some small defects on the bed while enjoying more surface contact area for better plate adhesion.

Some manufacturers recommend a first layer height that matches the diameter of the nozzle, which is mostly 0.3mm or 0.4mm (check your printer documentation).

Width factor is also important. The more material touching the bed the better. A value of 200% is usually recommended.

We have talked about thickness and layers previously. You want to know that FDM printing involves depositing one layer over another. Therefore, there is an inherent weak point where each layer is joined. The bad thing about this is that there is no way you can avoid it.

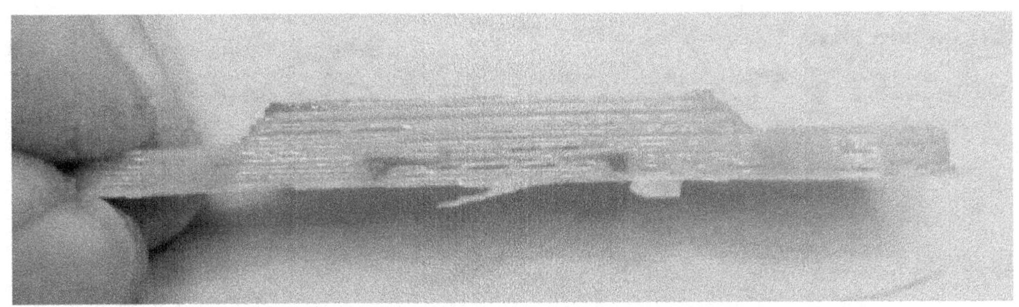

The more layers you use the smoother surface you can have, and the more weak points you will have as well!

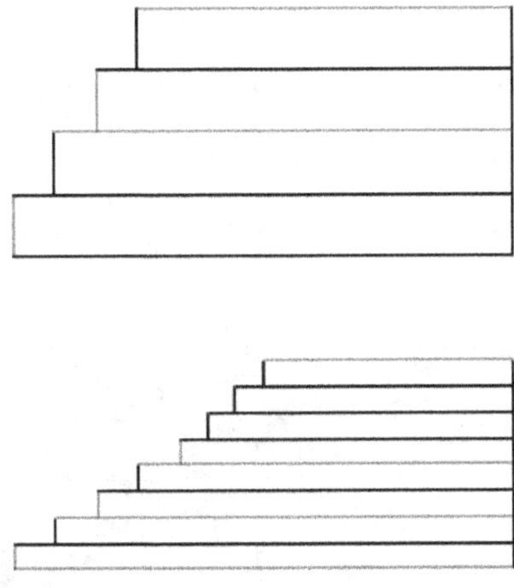

You may not be able to control how many layers are to be deposited by the printer, but you can have a rough estimate. If the layer height is 0.25mm and the desired thickness is 0.5mm, at least 2 layers will be required. It is simple math.

If structural strength is a concern, you may try to rotate your object from within the slicer software so that layering is done differently for the object. Layering is always slice by slice with one on top of another, so how the object sits on the bed directly determines how it is sliced and layered! Again, extensive testing would be required to determine what is best for your model strength-wise.

As you can see from the photo below, the layers/slices are pretty visible:

If adhesion is still poor, you should enable build plate adhesion from within the slicer so a wider contact surface will be printed for better stickiness. A larger contact surface will for sure adhere better to the bed. The larger the better...

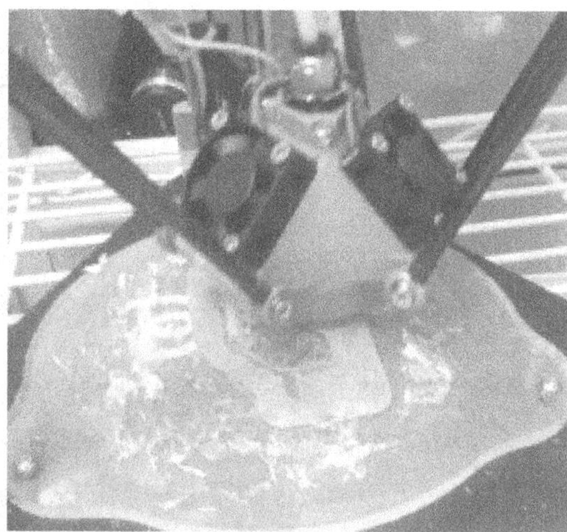

Build plate adhesion is in fact one of the most critical concepts in FDM 3D printing, and understanding why it helps requires looking at the physical forces acting on a print while it is being created. In short, build plate adhesion keeps the first layer of your print firmly attached to the bed, preventing warping, shifting, and complete detachment during the printing process. Without proper adhesion, even a perfectly sliced model will fail.

To understand why adhesion is so important, consider what happens inside a 3D printer during a print. The nozzle extrudes molten plastic at temperatures typically between two hundred and two hundred sixty degrees Celsius. As this plastic is laid down, it begins to cool immediately. Cooling causes the plastic to contract slightly, and this contraction creates internal stresses within the part. For a tall or wide print, these stresses can become substantial. If the first layer is not strongly bonded to the build plate, the contracting forces from the upper layers will literally pull the edges of the print upward, a defect known as warping or curling. Once the edge lifts off the bed, the nozzle may collide with the raised section on subsequent passes, knocking the entire print loose or causing layer shifts. Build plate adhesion directly counteracts these forces by anchoring the first layer firmly in place.

Another way adhesion helps is by providing stability during the printing process itself. As the print head moves back and forth, it exerts lateral forces on the part. The nozzle drags slightly against already extruded plastic, and rapid directional changes create vibrations. A poorly adhered print can slide, tilt, or rock on the build plate under these forces, especially for tall, narrow objects with a small footprint. Good adhesion keeps the print locked in position, ensuring that every layer is deposited exactly where it is supposed to be. Without this stability, even minimal movement will produce layer misalignment, resulting in a skewed or failed print.

Build plate adhesion also matters for the very first moments of the print. The initial extrusion must bond to the bed surface before any further layers are added. If the first line of plastic does not stick, subsequent lines will have nothing to attach to. This is why printers typically lay down a skirt, which is a line printed around the perimeter of the part, or a brim, which is a thin extension of the first layer outward from the part, or a raft, which is a temporary grid beneath the part. These adhesion aids increase the surface area in contact with the bed, providing a more secure anchor. A skirt helps prime the nozzle and confirms that the bed is level, while a brim adds a ring of material around the base of the part to resist warping at the edges. A raft creates an entire sacrificial layer underneath the part, which is particularly useful for parts with very small contact areas or for materials that are notoriously difficult to stick to the bed.

The material being printed also determines how much adhesion help is needed. PLA adheres relatively easily to common surfaces like heated glass, BuildTak, or PEI sheets, and often requires only a clean bed and a skirt to succeed. PETG is moderately easy but can be too aggressive on some surfaces, actually bonding so strongly that it damages the bed, so adhesion aids like brims must be used carefully. ABS and nylon, by contrast, are notorious for warping and require significant adhesion assistance, including a heated bed, an enclosure to maintain uniform temperature, and often a generous brim or a raft. Flexible TPU adheres very well to many surfaces but can be difficult to remove, so adhesion aids for TPU are more about controlling the first layer than about preventing warping.

Temperature also plays a role in adhesion. A heated bed helps the first layer stay warm longer, reducing the thermal shock that causes immediate contraction and lifting. For materials like ABS, a bed temperature of one hundred to one hundred ten degrees Celsius is common, while PLA typically uses sixty degrees. However, even with a heated bed, the edges of a large flat print may still cool faster than the center, creating stress that pulls the corners upward. A brim or raft counteracts this by distributing the contraction force over a wider area, essentially giving the edges more material to resist lifting.

Finally, proper bed preparation works together with adhesion aids. A clean, oil-free surface is essential, as fingerprints or dust will prevent plastic from sticking. Common adhesion assistants like glue stick, painter's tape, or specialized sprays create a textured or chemically receptive surface that the plastic can grip. These are not substitutes for a brim or raft but rather complementary techniques. The combination of a clean bed, appropriate temperature, good first layer squish, and a proper adhesion aid like a brim or raft provides the strongest possible foundation for a successful print.

Another trick is to apply a thin layer of glue to the bed surface right before printing. The primary way this works is by providing a consistent, slightly tacky surface for the first layer of plastic to grip onto. A clean glass or metal bed can be very smooth, and some materials, like ABS, contract significantly as they cool, causing corners to lift off a slick surface. The glue acts as a microscopic intermediate layer that bonds well to both the bed and the filament, holding the print firmly in place throughout the process. There are also practical benefits that make glue sticks a favorite among hobbyists. A well-known example is the purple-to-clear glue stick, which shows you exactly where you have applied the glue with its purple color, then dries clear, so you know precisely when the bed is ready for printing. The adhesive is also water-soluble, which makes cleaning the bed after a print very simple, as a rinse with water or a wipe with a damp cloth is usually all that is needed.

Regular paper glue should suffice in most cases.

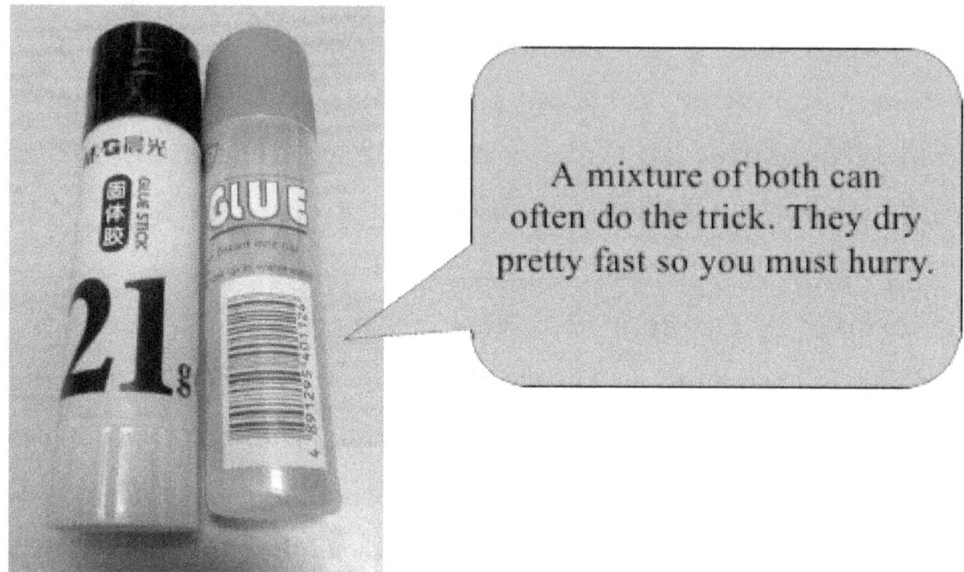

Retraction involves pulling back the filament from the nozzle and stop extrusion when there are discontinuous surfaces (such as holes) in the object.

This feature is by default enabled on almost all printers as it can reduce oozing. This is in fact a critical setting in FDM 3D printing that directly addresses one of the most common print defects, stringing. In simple terms, retraction pulls the filament backward inside the Bowden tube or direct drive extruder whenever the printer finishes one section of the print and must move, or travel, to a different location to start extruding again. By reversing the filament motion, retraction relieves the pressure inside the hot end and pulls the molten plastic away from the nozzle tip, preventing it from dripping or oozing out during the travel move.

To understand what retraction accomplishes, imagine the hot end as a syringe filled with molten plastic. Even after you stop pushing the plunger, some material will continue to dribble out of the needle because of residual pressure and gravity. In a 3D printer, this dribble manifests as thin, wispy strings of plastic that stretch across the open space between two separate parts of the print or between two features on the same part. These strings are purely cosmetic defects when mild, but in severe cases they can accumulate into thick blobs that the nozzle then drags through the print, causing surface scarring or even knocking the part off the build plate. Enabling retraction directly eliminates or dramatically reduces this oozing by actively pulling the molten column of plastic back up into the cooler part of the nozzle, creating a vacuum that stops the drip.

The effectiveness of retraction depends on several settings that work together. The retraction distance determines how far the filament is pulled back, typically between half a millimeter for direct drive extruders, where the motor is mounted directly above the nozzle, and five to seven millimeters for Bowden extruders, where the motor is mounted on the frame and pushes filament through a long tube. Bowden setups require longer retraction distances because there is more slack and flexibility in the long tube. The retraction speed controls how quickly the filament is pulled back, with faster speeds generally producing sharper cuts and cleaner stops, although too fast can cause the filament to strip or grind against the drive gear. Additional settings like retraction prime speed and extra prime amount control how the filament is pushed back into the nozzle when extrusion resumes, ensuring that the next line starts without a gap.

Beyond preventing stringing, enabling proper retraction also improves overall surface quality and dimensional accuracy. Without retraction, the nozzle will often leave small zits or blobs at the points where travel moves begin and end, because the oozed plastic accumulates and gets deposited when extrusion restarts. These surface imperfections are particularly visible on smooth, curved surfaces or on the outer perimeters of a print. A well-tuned retraction setting eliminates these blobs, producing cleaner seams and smoother walls. Additionally, reducing oozing means less post-processing work, as the user does not need to pick off strings or sand away blobs.

However, enabling retraction is not without trade-offs. Setting the retraction distance too high can pull molten plastic too far up into the cold zone of the hot end, where it solidifies and creates a clog or jam. This is especially problematic with materials that have a low melt viscosity or that crystallize quickly, such as PETG or certain nylons. Setting the retraction speed too high can cause the extruder motor to skip steps or grind a flat spot into the filament, particularly with flexible materials like TPU which compress rather than retract cleanly. For this reason, flexible filaments often require very short, slow retractions or even no retraction at all. Similarly, excessively frequent retractions on a model with many small segments can cause the filament to be worked back and forth repeatedly, wearing it down or inducing heat creep that softens the filament above the heat break.

Despite these trade-offs, enabling retraction with properly tuned settings is one of the most impactful improvements a user can make to print quality. A printer that leaves long spiderwebs between towers and a printer that produces clean, string-free results are often separated not by hardware differences but by whether retraction is enabled and correctly configured. Modern slicers enable retraction by default with sensible baseline values, typically two to three millimeters at forty millimeters per second for Bowden setups and zero point five to one millimeter at thirty millimeters per second for direct drive. From these baselines, users can print a simple retraction calibration tower to fine-tune the exact distance and speed for their specific filament, extruder, and hot end combination. The result of properly enabled retraction is cleaner prints, less post-processing, and fewer failed prints caused by oozing and blobbing.

Shell VS Infill

The shell is the outer wall of the object. Infill, on the other hand, is the partially hollow interior. A "thicker" wall is of course better structural-wise.

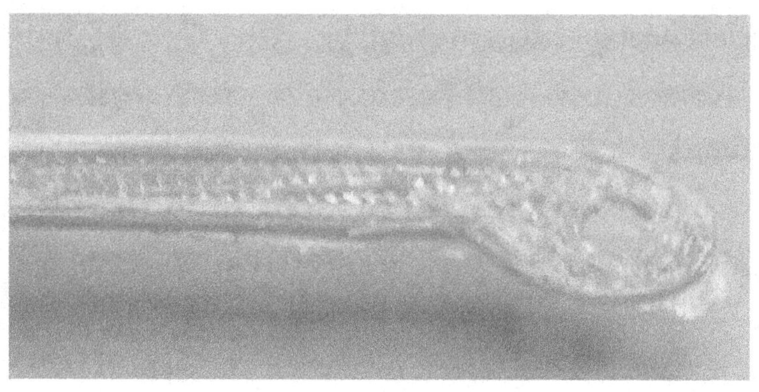

Shell Thickness

12   mm

Spiral Vase
☐

In Vase Mode the print will progress upward in a spiral relying on smooth and continuous movements of the Z-axis. It is particularly useful for printing container objects.

Infill Pattern determines how the partially hollow interior of a 3d model is filled up. The reason the interior is not entirely solid is to save filament and time. Making an object 100% solid can be very costly.

The infill is invisible to you. Typically the infill has a pattern of grid or honeycomb. Grid is very common.

If your 3d model is not required to do anything structural, it should not matter much and the default should suffice.

INFILL

Fill Density

20   %

If your model is a structural part, different patterns may produce different strength. Do note that these patterns are inside the model – they are not visible to you at all.

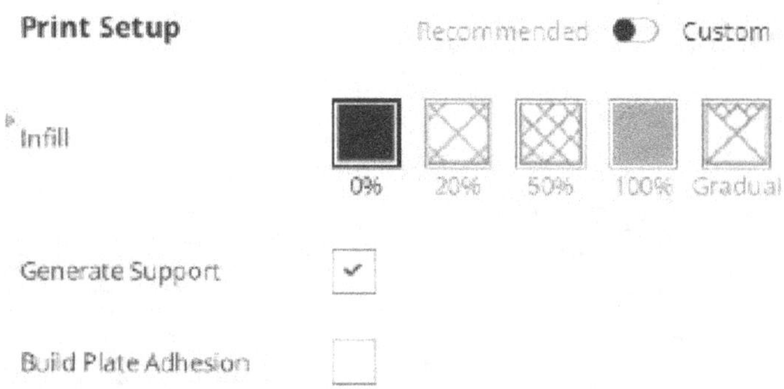

Fill Density is a parameter in percentage you can specify. Higher density means more rigid structure. It will also consume more printing material. A density of 0% means hollow. A 20% density is typically good for printing a prototype.

When there is too little infill, there will be plenty of air gap in the interior. When you attempt to print a solid top over it, problems may occur (weak structure, visible gap on the surface,...etc).

INFILL

Fill Density

20 %

Bottom/Top Thickness

0.8 mm

This is one tricky thing to pay attention to. If your object has a semi hollow interior but there is a solid top that sits on it, the fill density of the infill should not be set too low.

A solid top without sound support can collapse easily.

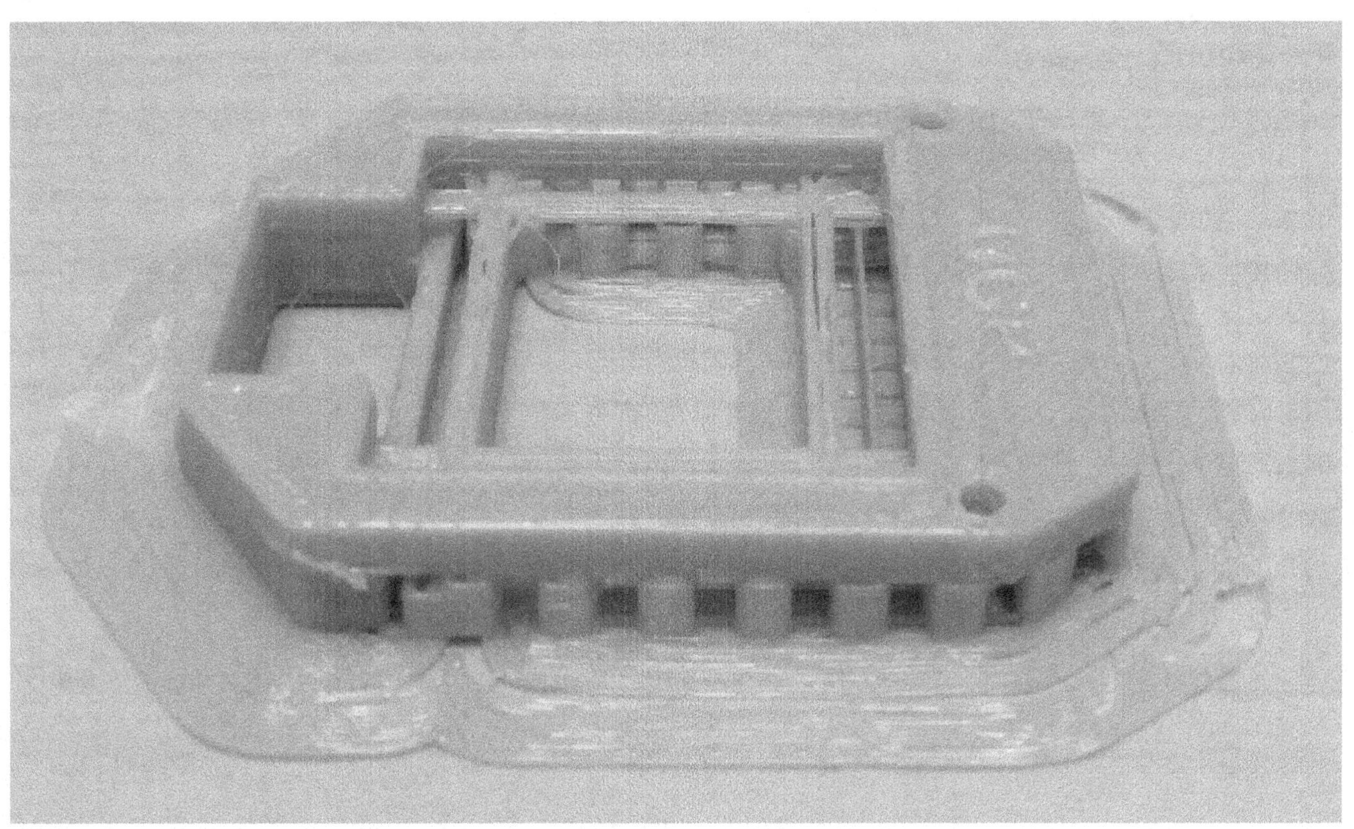

To avoid visible gaps at the top and bottom of the final printout, the thickness should be set to at least 0.5mm. And you should always go for solid top and solid bottom.

TOP & BOTTOM LAYERS

Cut off Object Bottom

Solid Top
☑

Solid Bottom
☑

Proper support

A raft is a horizontal grid under your object. It serves as a platform that sticks to the bed. A brim is like a platform surrounding the bottom of your object (but without having anything under your object). They both aim to improve stickiness to the bed.

You can configure the number of brim lines which are the contour lines in the brim. The more the stronger. Generally the default value will do just fine.

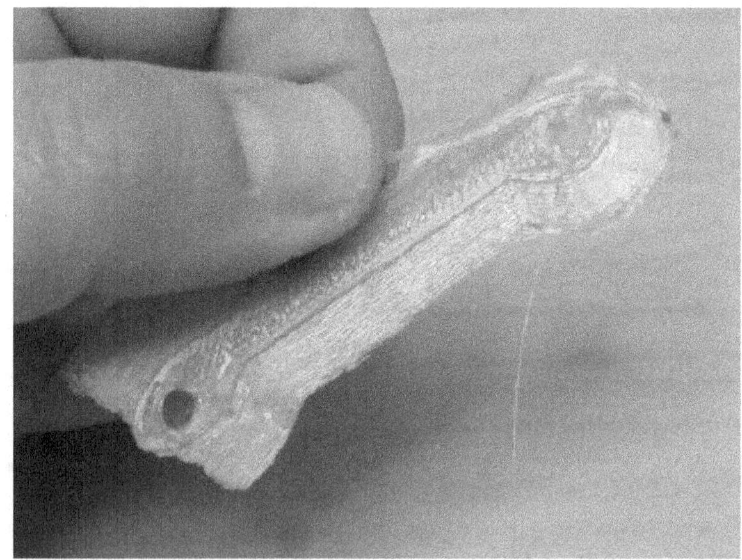

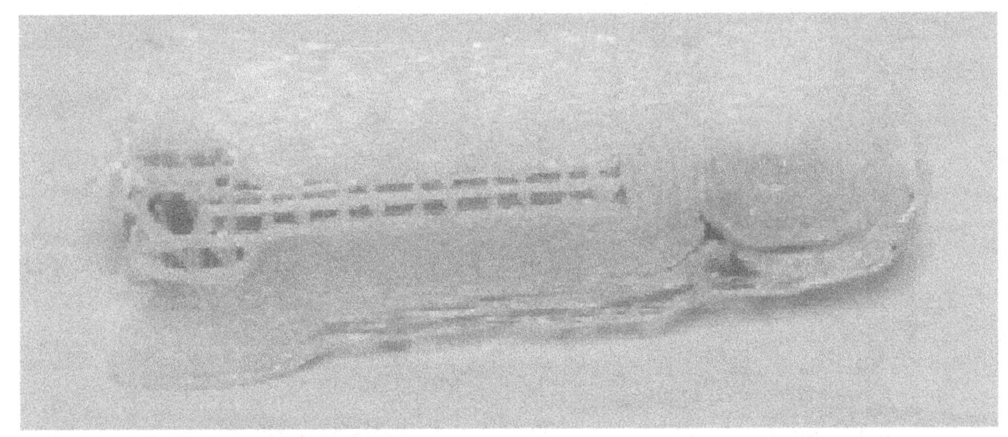

Any surface that touches the brim or raft will not be smooth so further processing will be required.

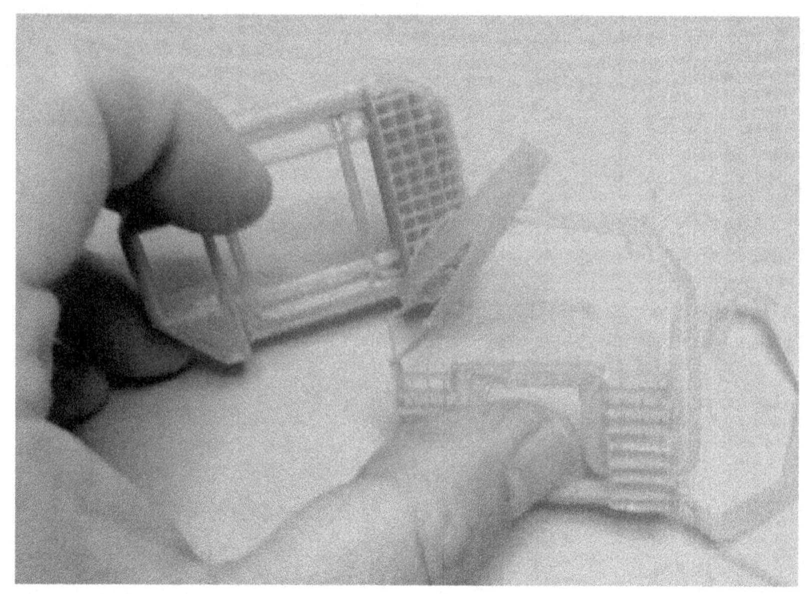

A skirt serves a slightly different purpose. It is a line of material surrounding but not attached to your object. It is usually printed first prior to your object. You use it to allow the print head to kinda warm up and normalize the material flow, and to test print something so to find out if plate adhesion is good.

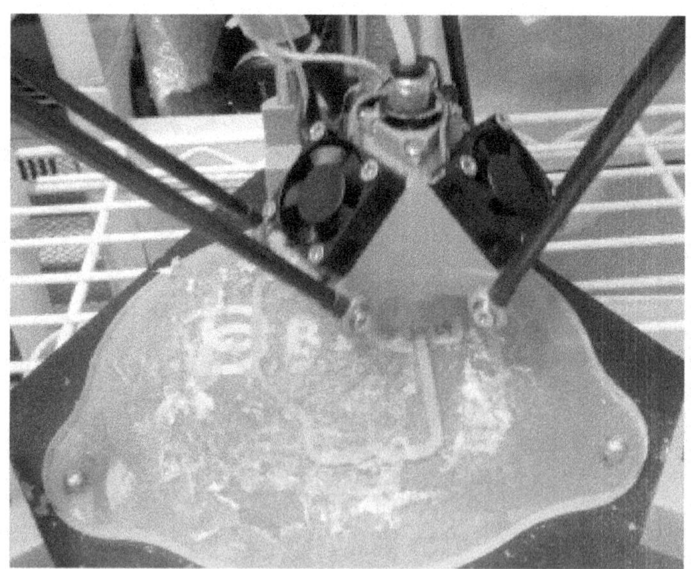

You will need to have proper support when the object to print has empty areas at the bottom or when there are overhangs. Printing large holes will also require support so to prevent the material from collapsing along the print process.

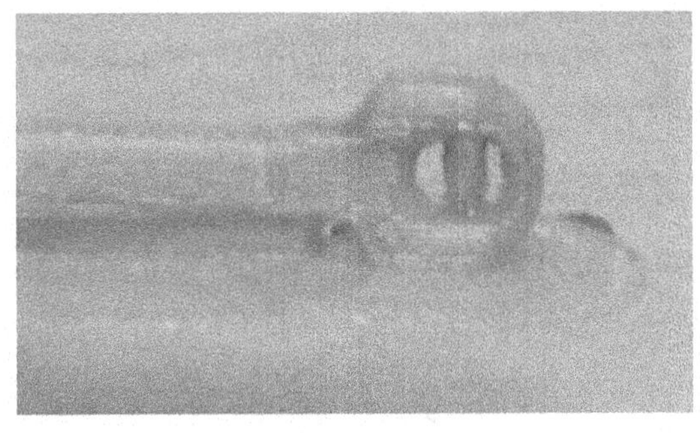
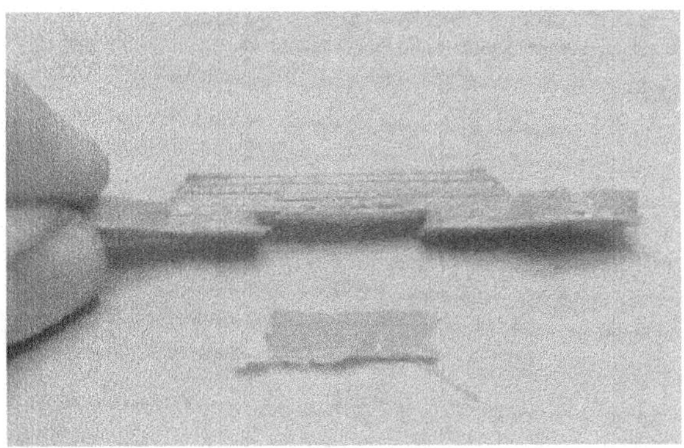

If your object has many empty spaces, holes, overhangs and bridges throughout the object body, when setting the Support option you should choose Everywhere. Otherwise you may want all supports to be originated from the bed. Supports that actually stand on the bed (i.e. touching the build plate) are usually more reliable.

SUPPORT MATERIAL

Support

Touching Build Plate

None

Touching Build Plate

Everywhere

Support Type

Lines

Grid

Lines

You also need to know the concept of YHT. Both letter Y and letter T have overhangs at the top. The letter H, in contrast, has a bridge in the middle.

Generally, overhangs less than 45 degrees may not require support. Bridge less than 5mm in length may also not require support. Talking about the type of support, grid is stronger than lines. However, it will take longer to finish printing.

Your slicer software may be smart enough to prepare the necessary support for you. If not, you may need to include some support elements in your model design. In fact this is a recommended approach if your aged slicer software does not really have the necessary intelligence to generate proper support for complicated models.

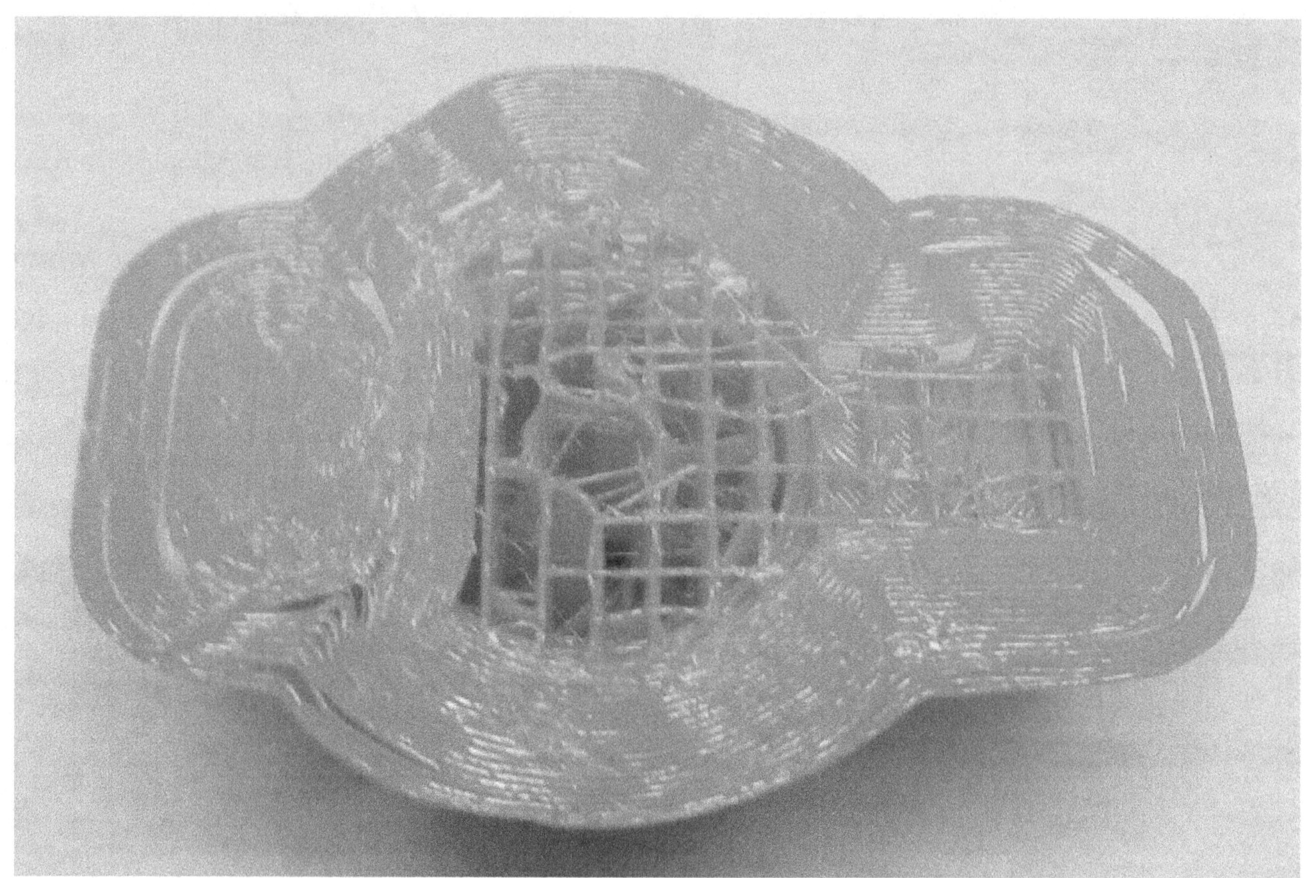

Support is not always necessary, and in fact, a well-designed print often requires no support at all. Knowing when to enable supports and when to leave them disabled is a skill that separates beginner from experienced 3D printing, as unnecessary supports waste material, increase print time, and leave rough surfaces where the supports were attached.

The reason supports are sometimes necessary comes down to gravity and the way FDM printing builds objects layer by layer. Each new layer of plastic must be deposited onto something solid that exists below it. If a feature extends outward horizontally with nothing beneath it, the molten plastic will simply droop or fall into empty space. This is known as an overhang. The angle of the overhang determines whether support is needed. Vertical walls have zero degrees of overhang and need no support. Shallow overhangs up to about forty-five degrees from vertical are generally printable without support because each new layer overlaps sufficiently with the layer below. As the overhang angle becomes more extreme, approaching horizontal at ninety degrees, the nozzle would essentially be extruding into thin air, and support becomes absolutely necessary. The general rule of thumb is that angles steeper than about fifty to sixty degrees from vertical, or flatter than thirty to forty degrees from horizontal, begin to require support for reliable printing.

Several factors influence exactly when support becomes necessary. A smaller layer height, such as 0.1 millimeters instead of 0.2 millimeters, allows for gentler overhangs because each step upward is shallower, giving the plastic more overlap with the previous layer. Better part cooling also improves overhang performance, as a powerful fan directed precisely at the nozzle tip can solidify the extruded plastic almost instantly, allowing it to bridge short gaps and maintain shape even at steeper angles. Wide extrusion widths relative to layer height also help, as a wider, flatter bead of plastic has more surface area to grip the layer below. Conversely, a printer with poor cooling or a very high layer height will require supports for even moderate overhangs that a well-tuned machine could print unaided.

There is also an entire class of geometries called bridges that can often print without supports. A bridge is a horizontal span connecting two raised points, like the top of a doorway. When the nozzle moves straight across the gap, it stretches the molten plastic between the two anchor points. With adequate cooling and proper settings, the plastic solidifies quickly enough to form a taut, straight line across the gap. Short bridges of a few millimeters are very easy, while longer bridges of several centimeters become challenging and may require supports at their midpoints. However, even long bridges can be improved by adding a single thin support tower in the center rather than a full dense support structure beneath the entire span.

Despite these capabilities, there are many situations where supports are genuinely necessary. Features like downward-facing flat surfaces, holes that are parallel to the build plate, and sharp inside corners with no lower support will always droop or sag without supports. Similarly, models with detailed undersides, such as the chin of a bust or the inside of an arch, will require support unless the model is reoriented on the build plate. This last point is critical, because the decision to use supports is not just about the model design but also about how the model is rotated. A model that would require extensive supports when printed standing upright might require no supports at all when printed lying on its side or at a forty-five degree angle. For example, a benchy boat is designed specifically to test overhang performance without supports, as its hull, roof, and wheelhouse all feature progressively steeper angles that should print cleanly on a well-calibrated machine. But if that same benchy were printed upside down, it would require massive support structures for every feature.

Choosing to use supports also comes with significant trade-offs. Supports consume filament that does not become part of the final object, increasing material cost and waste. They add substantial print time, sometimes doubling or tripling the duration for models with complex overhangs. Most importantly, supports leave behind rough surfaces where they were attached, regardless of how carefully they are tuned. The interface between the support and the model is always a weak point, and removing supports often leaves scars, tiny bumps, or broken details, especially on delicate features. Dissolvable supports made from PVA or HIPS can eliminate the scarring issue by washing away in water or a chemical bath, but these materials require a dual-extruder printer and add significant complexity and cost.

Everything about the print head

The extruder is the print head. The extrusion process is in fact a process of print flow, NOT print move. Keeping proper flow means keeping the nozzle clean and unobstructed at all time. If the nozzle is badly clogged, replace it immediately. It is very cheap.

Many problems can occur at the print head. For Delta printer, there is no motor at the print head. There is a pass-through tube adapter, a metal brass surrounded by plastic casing, a steel throat and a nozzle attached to the heater block, and several motors. The photo below shows the heater block and the steel throat.

As previously said, nozzle is real cheap so if it is clogged you can simply replace it with a wrench. Or if you have the specialized needle tools you can try to punch through what is clogging the nozzle opening. They are available from 0.1 all the way up to 0.10 or beyond:

The tube adapter is also easily replaceable. If for whatever reason the PLA is broken half way then you will need to pull out the tube. Frequent pulling out and pushing in of the tube may break the adapter.

Different types of adapters are available but you need to choose one that works with 4mm PTFE tube if you are using 1.75mm PLA. And very importantly this must be a pass-through adapter allowing the entire tube to pass through it to reach the steel throat.

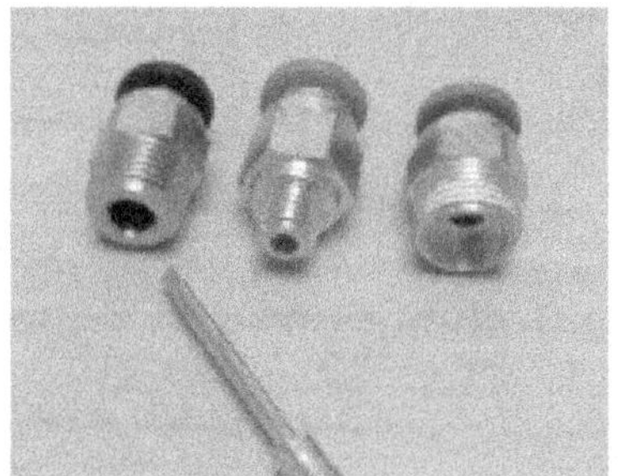

PTFE shorts for Poly Tetra Fluoro Ethylene. The 4mm we talk about is the outside diameter of the tube. We recommend that you use one that is clear so you can see through it and tell if anything goes wrong inside it.

If the heater wires are doomed, you will need to replace the whole set (including the heater cartridge and the thermistor).

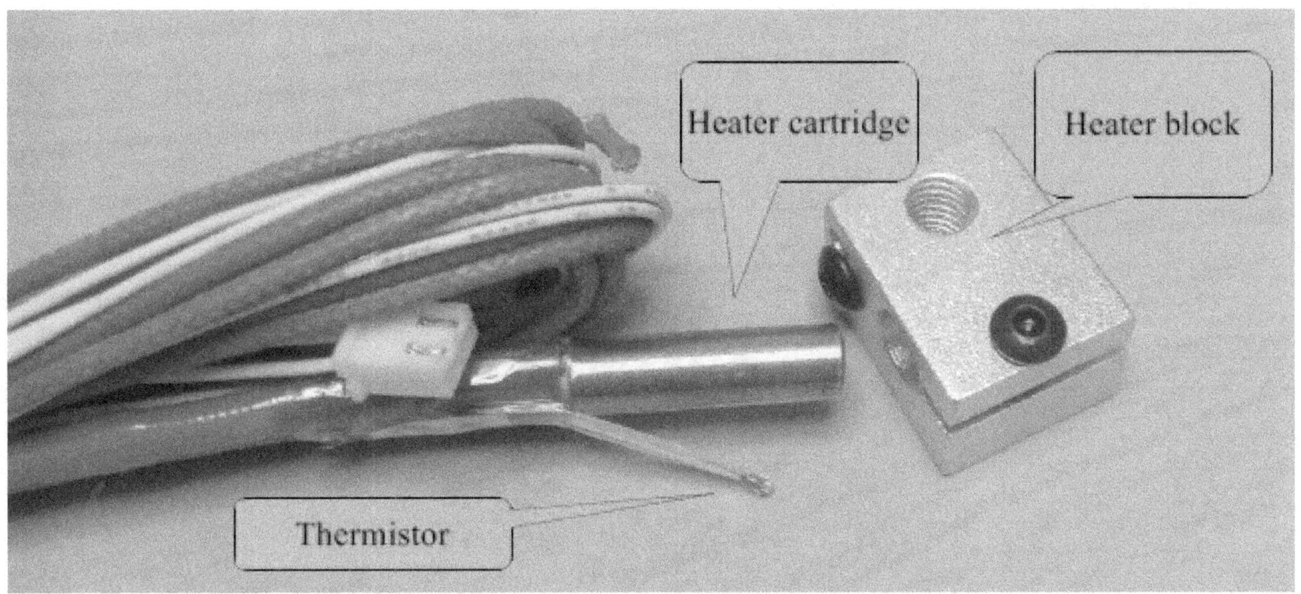

You may as well replace the heat block since it is cheap. You need a hex driver to tighten things up. The thermistor is small — you need to insert into the smaller hole and use the hex screw next to it to secure the wires.

The steel throat is on one end and the nozzle is on another. Use water seal tape around the thread of both.

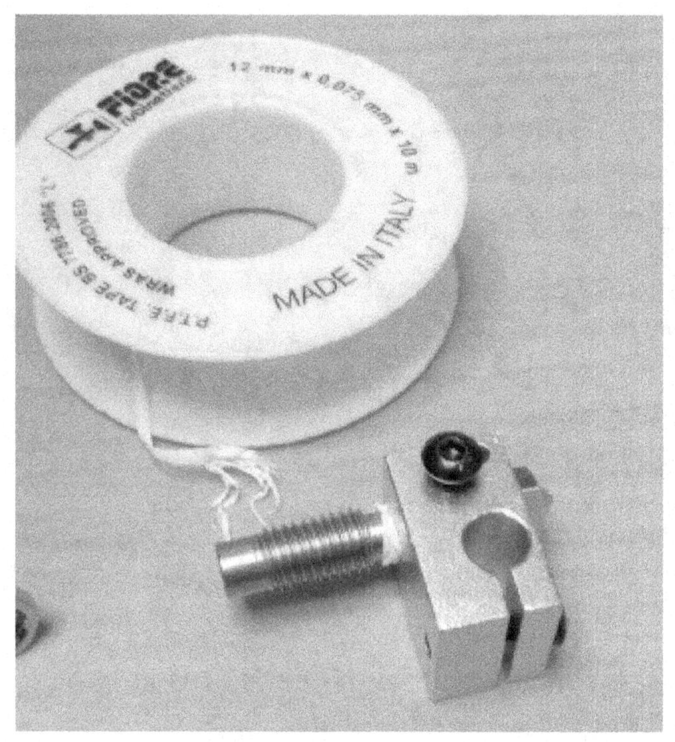

The nozzle stays on the side of the hex screw. It must be completely tightened prior to installing the steel throat.

The heat block itself does not necessarily need to be replaced regularly, but the components attached to it, particularly the nozzle and the thermistor, do. While the heater block is a durable chunk of metal designed to last for years, the parts that make contact with filament or manage temperature undergo constant stress and degradation during normal printing. However, when people discuss replacing the hotend, they are often referring to the entire assembly including the block, but the reasons typically point back to specific consumable parts.

To clarify, the heat block is the metal mass, usually aluminum, that holds the heater cartridge, the temperature sensor which is the thermistor, and the nozzle. Its main job is to store thermal energy to keep the temperature stable. Under normal conditions, this block does not wear out and does not need scheduled replacement. However, several critical components attached to or working with the block do wear out and require regular attention.

The nozzle is the primary consumable of the hotend. Standard brass nozzles are excellent heat conductors but are relatively soft. Even if you only print standard materials like PLA or PETG, the constant friction of the filament flowing through the tiny orifice will slowly erode the internal geometry over time. This leads to a larger, misshapen hole, which causes stringing, poor surface quality, and inconsistent extrusion. A good rule of thumb for brass nozzles is replacement every few kilograms of filament. This wear accelerates dramatically with abrasive materials like carbon fiber composites, glow in the dark filaments, or wood filled filaments, which can chew up a brass nozzle in less than fifty hours of printing. Upgrading to a stainless steel or hardened steel nozzle significantly extends this lifespan, with high quality steel nozzles potentially lasting around two thousand hours under normal use.

The thermistor, the small temperature sensor embedded in the heat block, is a surprisingly fragile component that degrades over time due to constant thermal cycling from repeated heating and cooling. A failing thermistor is a serious issue because it sends incorrect temperature data to the printer's control board. Symptoms include erratic temperature readings, sudden thermal runaway errors, or the printer failing to reach the target temperature, all of which will ruin prints and can be a safety hazard. If your printer's temperature display starts fluctuating wildly, the thermistor is likely the culprit and needs replacement. The heater cartridge, while less common than nozzle or thermistor failure, can also fail on heavily used printers. This component generates the heat, and over hundreds of hours of use, the internal wiring can degrade or the connection can become intermittent, leading to the printer failing to heat up or struggling to maintain temperature during prints.

Given that you generally replace components rather than the entire block, there are specific scenarios where replacing the whole block assembly is the best or only solution. The most common reason for a full hotend replacement is what users call the plastic blob of death. If a print fails and the plastic curls up and sticks to the nozzle, it can form a large, solid blob of plastic that completely encases the heat block, the thermistor wires, and the heater cartridge wires. Trying to chisel this hard plastic off without destroying the fragile, hair thin thermistor wires is nearly impossible, so in this case it is faster and safer to replace the entire hotend assembly including the block, heater, and thermistor with a new one.

Another scenario requiring full replacement is component incompatibility or upgrade. When replacing a failed thermistor or heater cartridge, you need to find the exact specifications. If the part is obsolete or you want to upgrade to a higher performance component like a fifty watt or sixty watt heater, it might be more straightforward to install a new, complete hotend kit.

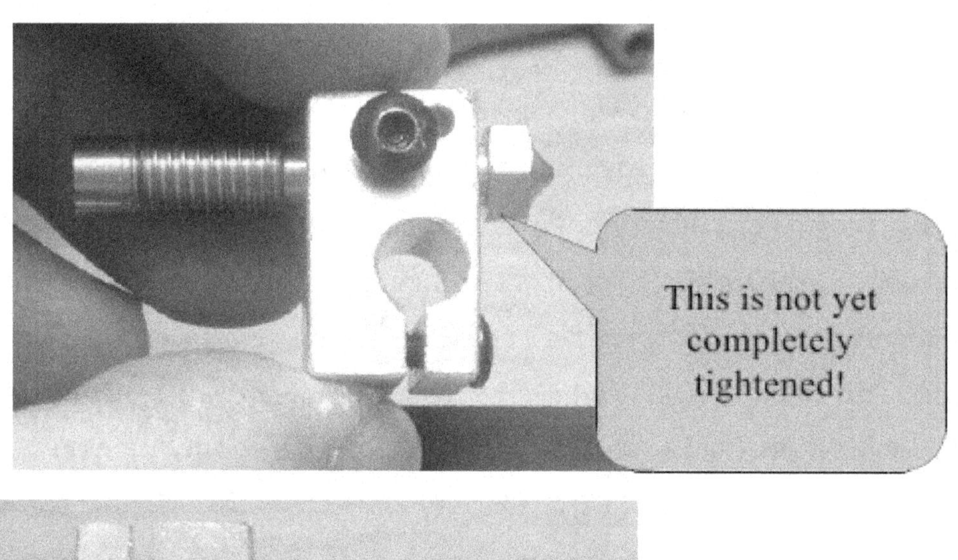

When installing the heat block be very gentle with the wires. These wires are not that strong and can break if getting twisted too much.

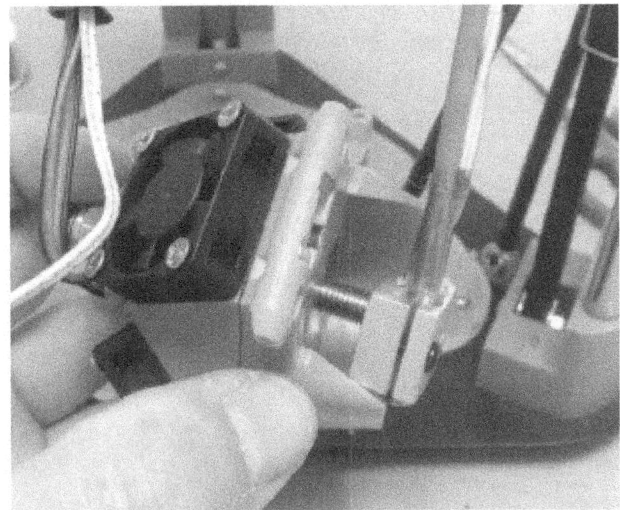 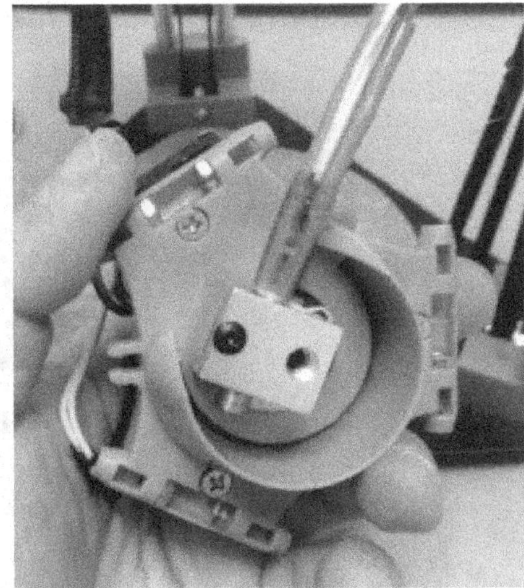

An easy approach would be to install and tighten up the heater block first before plugging in the heater cartridge and the thermistor.

 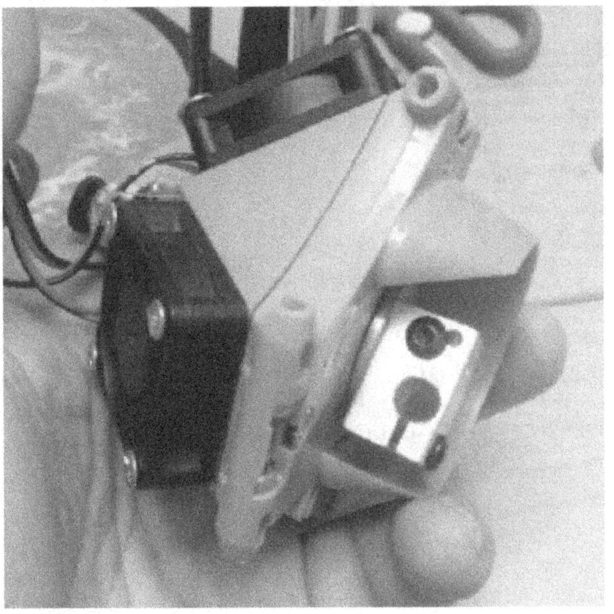

If your replacement heater block has a slightly different size, you may need to use a ring spacer in between so that it can be completely locked without any "play". The heater block MUST NOT be allowed to wobble!

The new wires do not have to pass through the existing protective wrap. You can wrap them externally as long as they do not get in the way of the print head movement. If the new wires are too long, use zip ties to tie them up somewhere at the top.

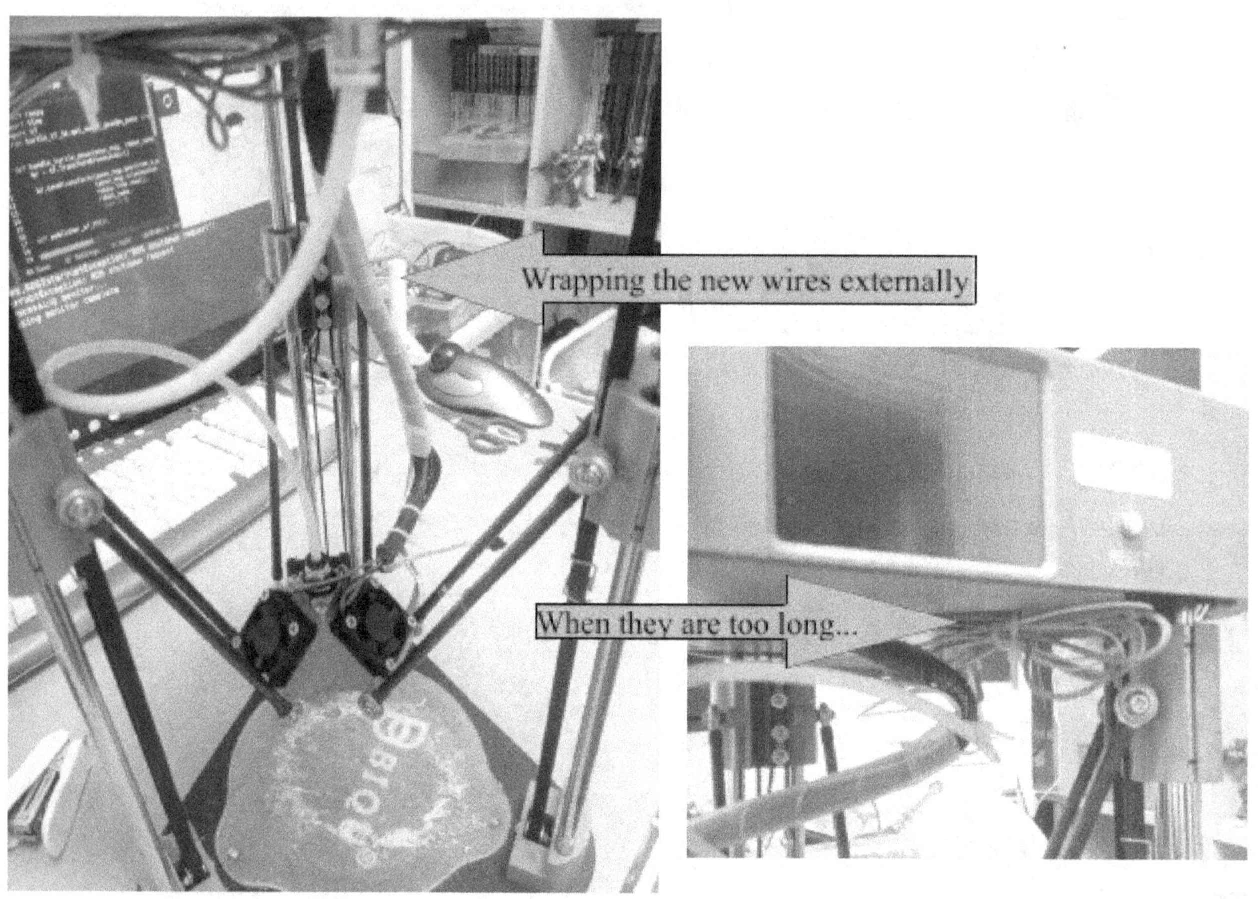

To connect the other end of the wires to the circuitry, you must remove the bottom plate of the top compartment.

The two heater wires are of the same color, meaning you do not need to worry about any mismatch.. The thermistor wires have a small connector plug so you won't be able to get wiring wrong neither.

Wiring can be inconvenient since the compartment is small. It is particularly uneasy to insert strand wires into the small hole of the connectors. You can use solid wires inside the compartment since they are much easier to handle. However, outside of the compartment where the wires have to move along with the print head you will have no choice but to use flexible strand wires.

For most users, regular maintenance is more important than frequent replacement. Using a small brass brush to clean melted plastic off the heat block, carefully avoiding the wires, while the nozzle is hot is a standard practice that prevents buildup and extends the life of the assembly. Furthermore, if you replace a nozzle or the entire hotend, you must perform a PID tune to recalibrate the temperature control algorithm and recalibrate your Z offset to account for the new nozzle's exact position to ensure safe and accurate printing. So while the heat block is a durable part that does not need routine replacement, paying attention to the nozzle, thermistor, and heater cartridge as consumables will keep your printer running reliably for years.

There are nozzle cleaning kits available:

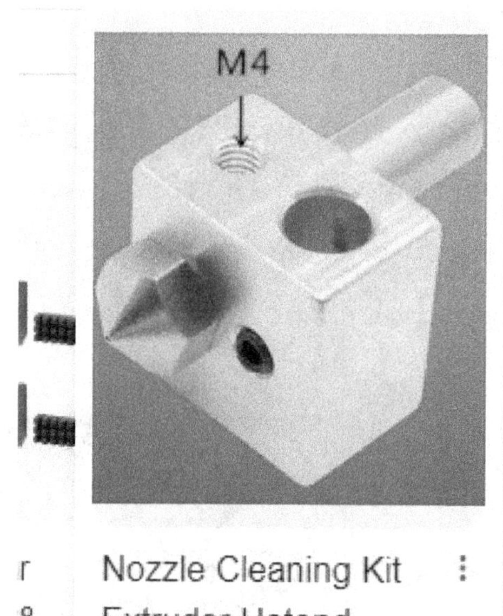

r   Nozzle Cleaning Kit   ⋮
&   Extruder Hotend
i...   Heater Block Set 3d
     Printer Part

£12.86

eBay - besidunte

Leveling

Whatever you have done to the print head, leveling has to be done after parts replacement so the fixed print head won't crash onto the bed. To understand why leveling is needed, one must first recognize that a Delta printer's motion system is based on parallel kinematics, where the print head's position is calculated by the firmware from the heights of three independent vertical carriages. The firmware uses mathematical formulas called inverse kinematics to determine exactly how high each carriage must be to position the nozzle at any given X, Y, Z coordinate. These formulas rely on several physical constants: the length of the diagonal arms, the radius of the towers around the build plate, the offset of the effector center from the carriages, and the exact positions of the endstops at the top of each tower. If any of these values is even slightly wrong, the firmware's calculation of where the nozzle is will be incorrect.

The most immediate consequence of poor calibration is that the nozzle will not maintain a consistent distance from the build plate as it moves across the bed. On a properly calibrated Delta, the nozzle stays perfectly level and at a constant Z height as it travels horizontally. On an uncalibrated Delta, the nozzle may dip down toward the bed at one edge and rise away from it at the opposite edge, or it may follow a wavy, uneven path as the arms move through their ranges. This manifests as inconsistent first layer adhesion, with the nozzle scraping the bed in some areas and printing in midair in others.

Another reason leveling is critical on a Delta printer is the issue of tower alignment. The three vertical rails must be perfectly parallel to one another and perfectly perpendicular to the build plate. If one tower leans slightly inward or outward, the arm attached to that carriage will reach further or shorter than expected, introducing a systematic error that changes with height. A leaning tower causes the effector to tilt and shift position as it moves near that tower, ruining accuracy for prints that extend to the edges of the build plate. Cartesian printers typically have simpler mechanical alignment requirements, but a Delta printer's calibration process actually measures and compensates for these tower misalignments by building a correction map.

Thermal expansion adds yet another layer of necessity to Delta leveling. As the printer heats up for a print, the aluminum or metal components expand at different rates. The build plate may rise slightly, the arms may lengthen, and the frame may change dimension. A Delta that was perfectly calibrated at room temperature may be significantly out of calibration at operating temperature for materials like ABS requiring a heated bed at one hundred degrees Celsius. For this reason, many Delta users perform their calibration when the printer is fully heated, probing the bed after it has reached printing temperature, to ensure that the calibration accounts for thermal expansion.

Follow the manul instructions of your printer to perform the appropriate levelling. The printer should come with a function that performs leveling for you. The process should not be a manual one. A special leveling sensor is needed for the Delta printer— you need to plug it into the nozzle when it is cooled down. As a quick tip, you may need to use a small piece of self sticking rubber (such as the Pritt Multifix) to help secure it in place (leveling requires print head movement and the sensor may fall off along the process)...

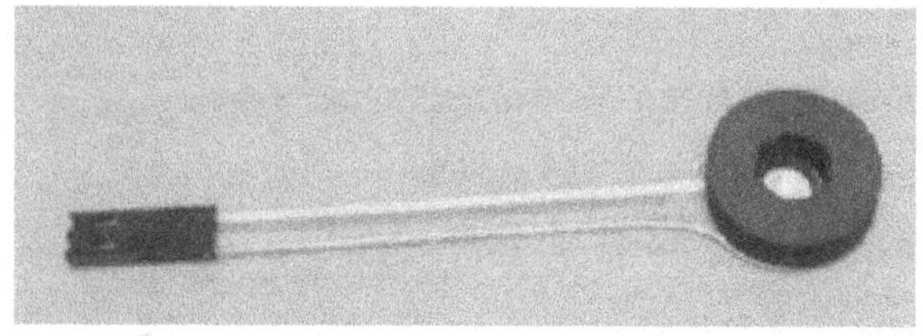

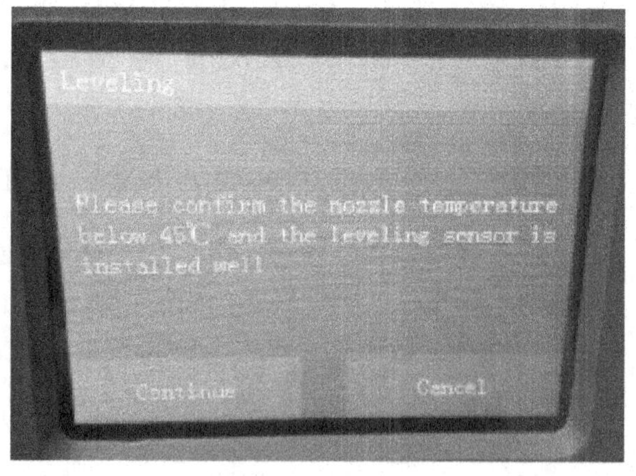

The leveling sensor is not merely a convenience for avoiding paper leveling, but a fundamental component that enables the machine to understand its own geometry. It measures the actual distances between the nozzle and the bed, solves for the printer's true mechanical constants, creates a detailed height map of the bed surface, and provides the Z offset needed for first layer printing. Without this sensor, a Delta owner would have to manually calibrate arm lengths, tower positions, endstop offsets, and bed flatness using trial and error and feeler gauges, a process so tedious and error prone that few users would ever achieve truly reliable printing.

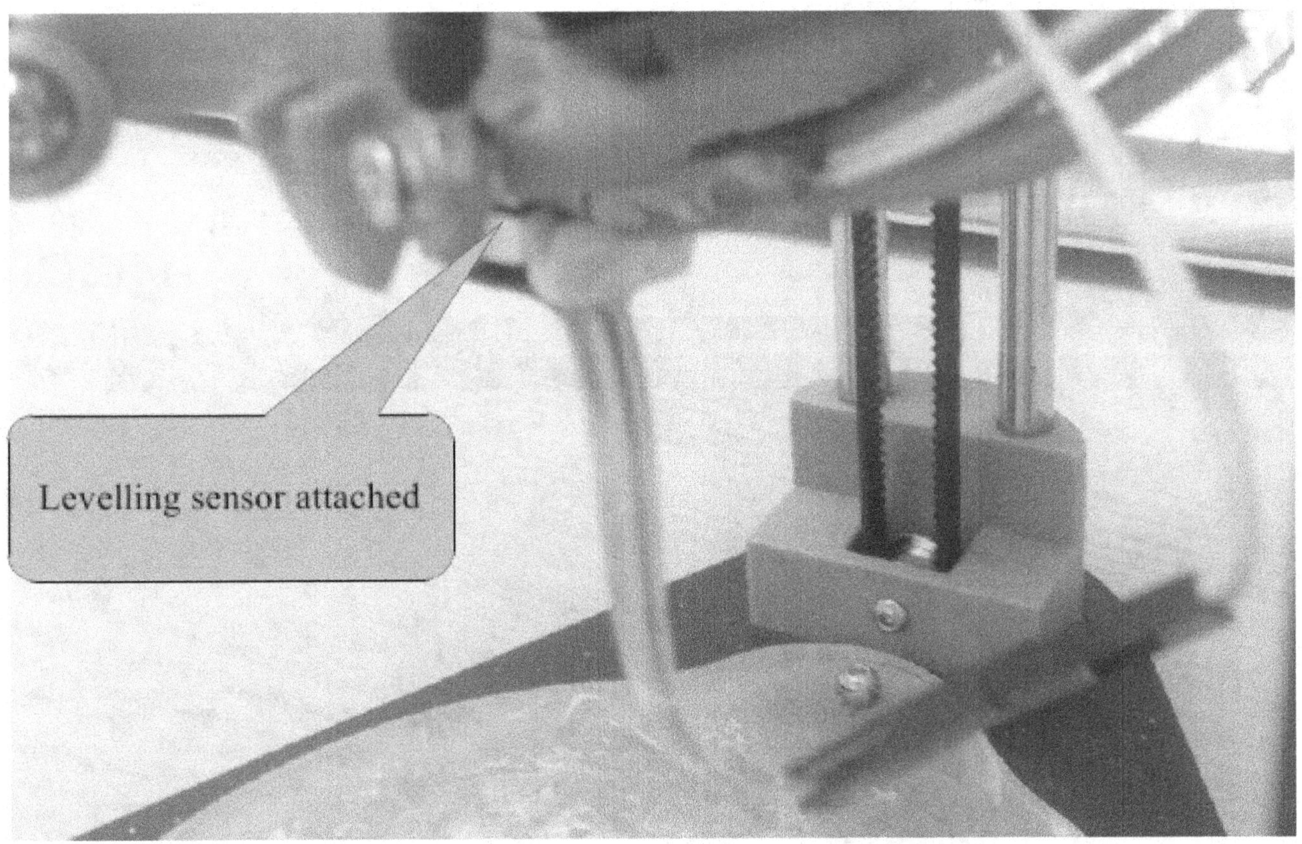

END OF BOOK

Please email your questions and comments to editor@hobbypress.net

Print your own parts for repair and upgrade!

UpgradePARTS.com has an extensive collection of free 3d models for airsoft guns, hobby models, drones and RC cars.

http://upgradeparts.com

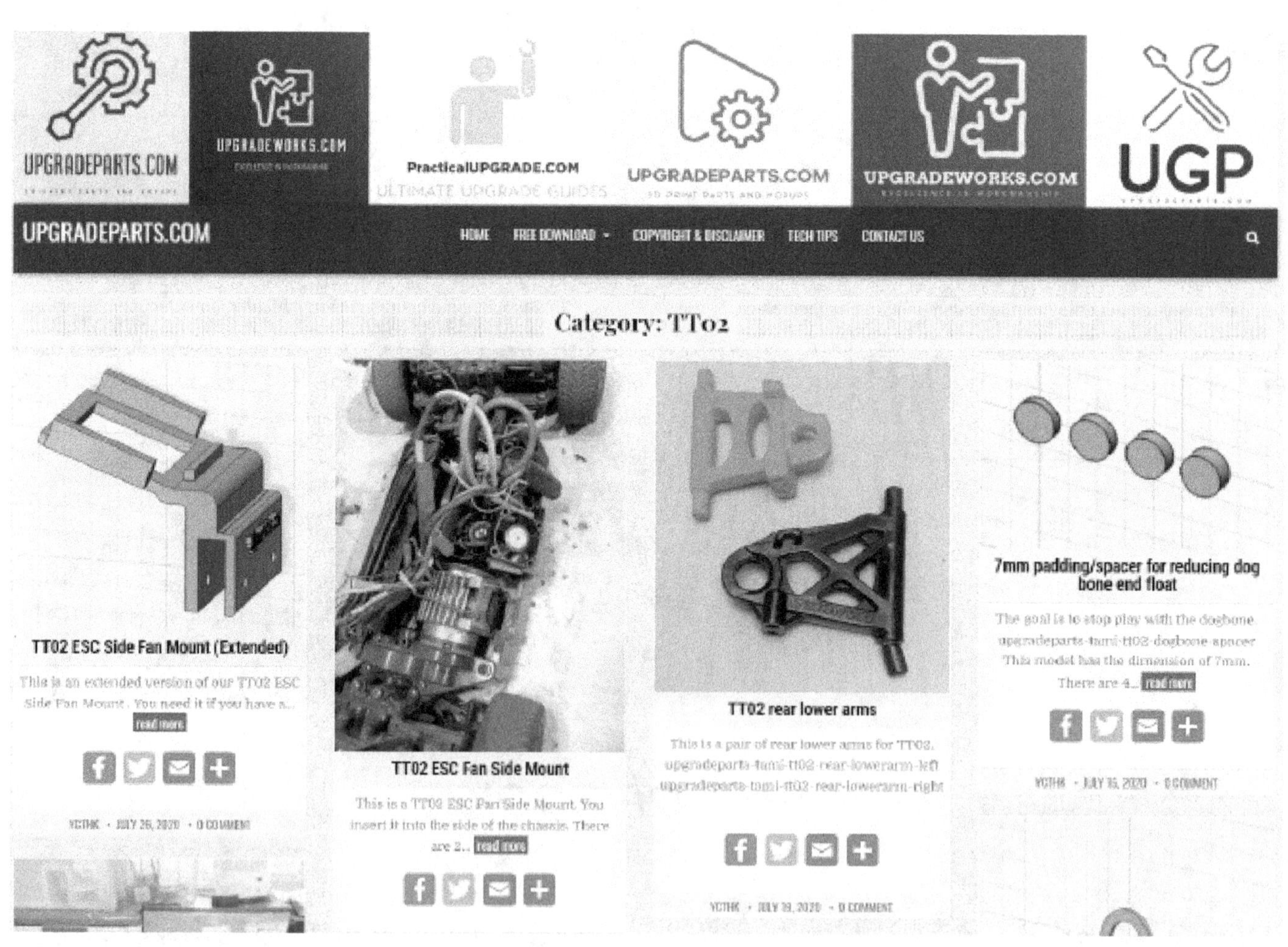

P. 92

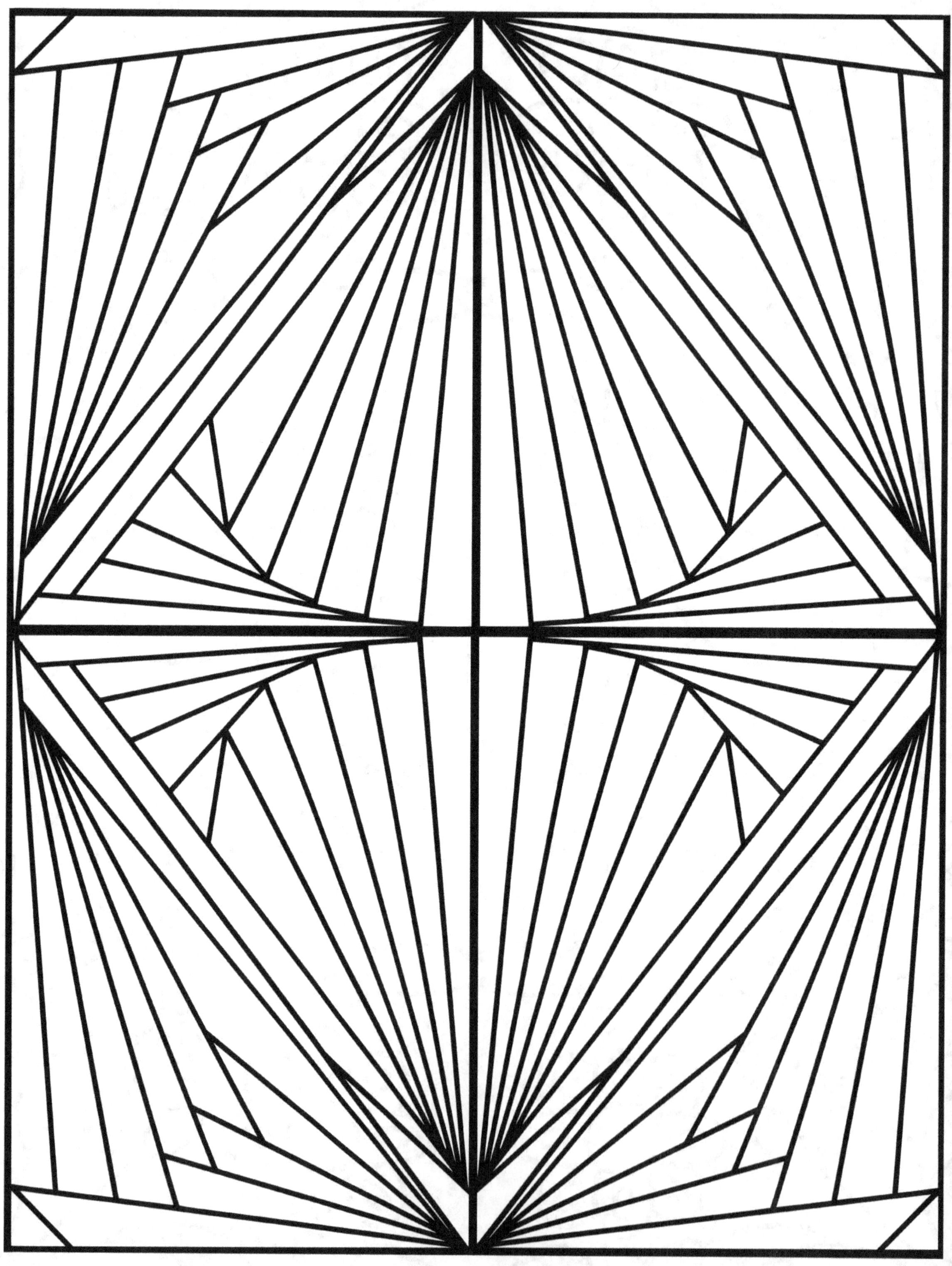

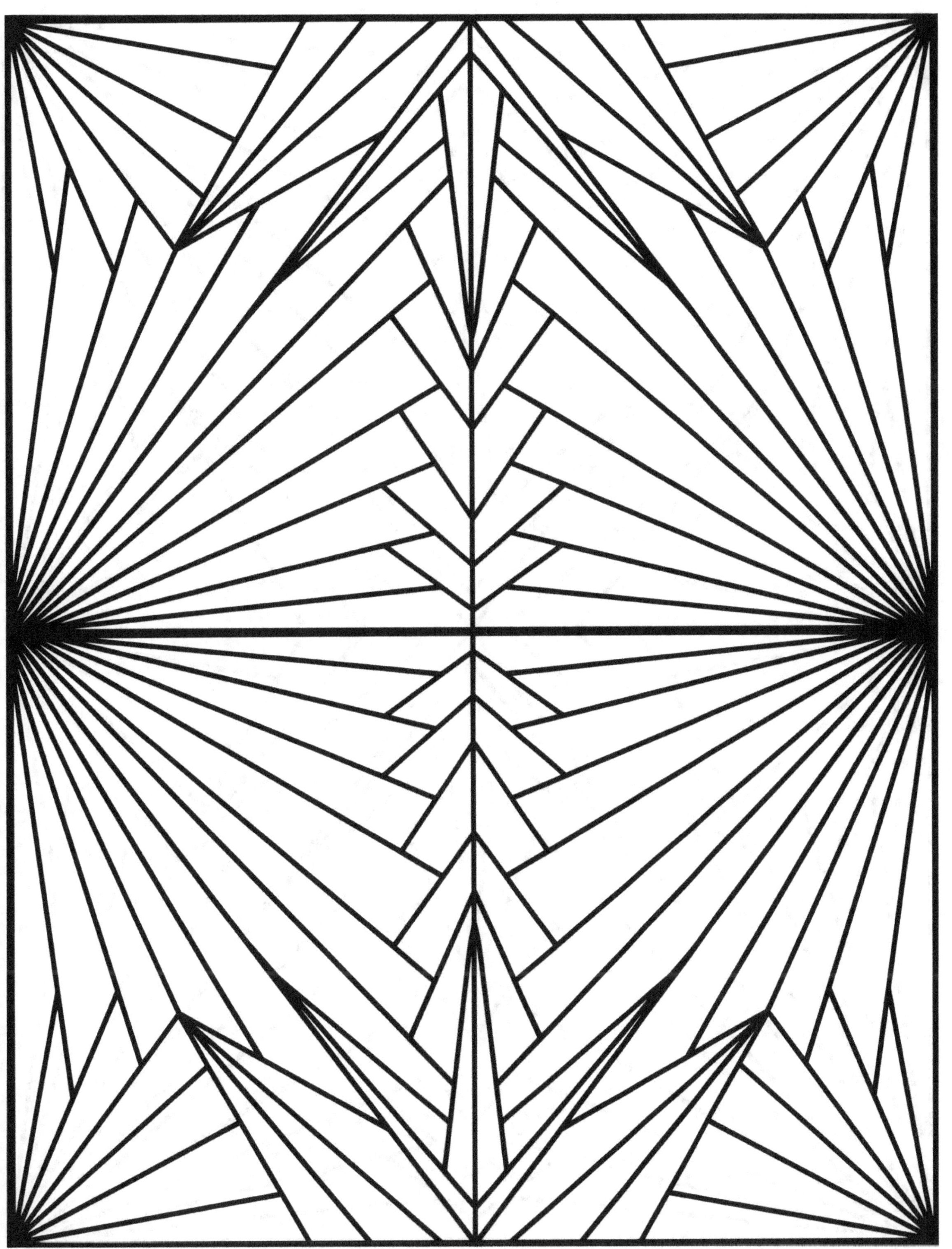

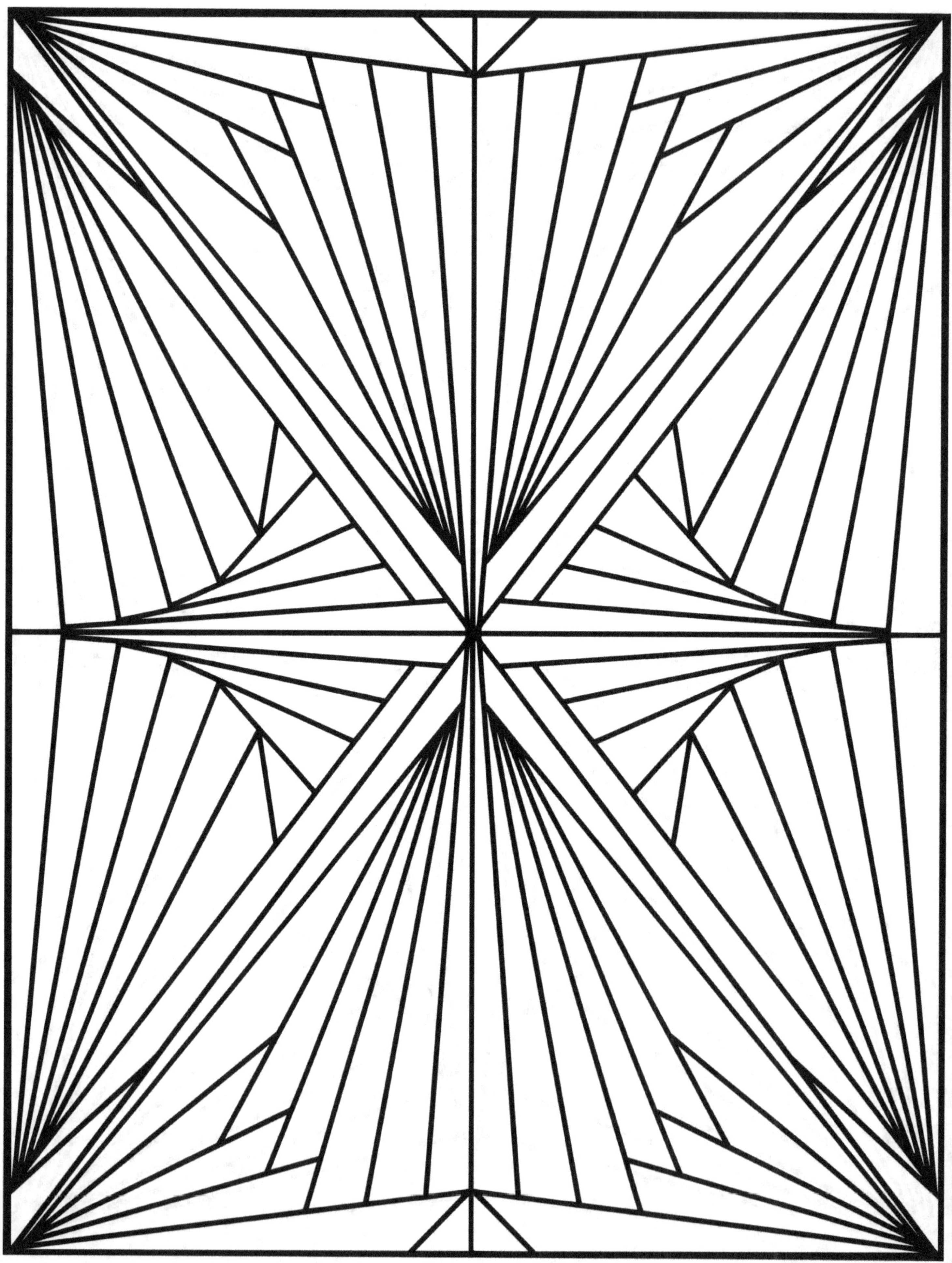

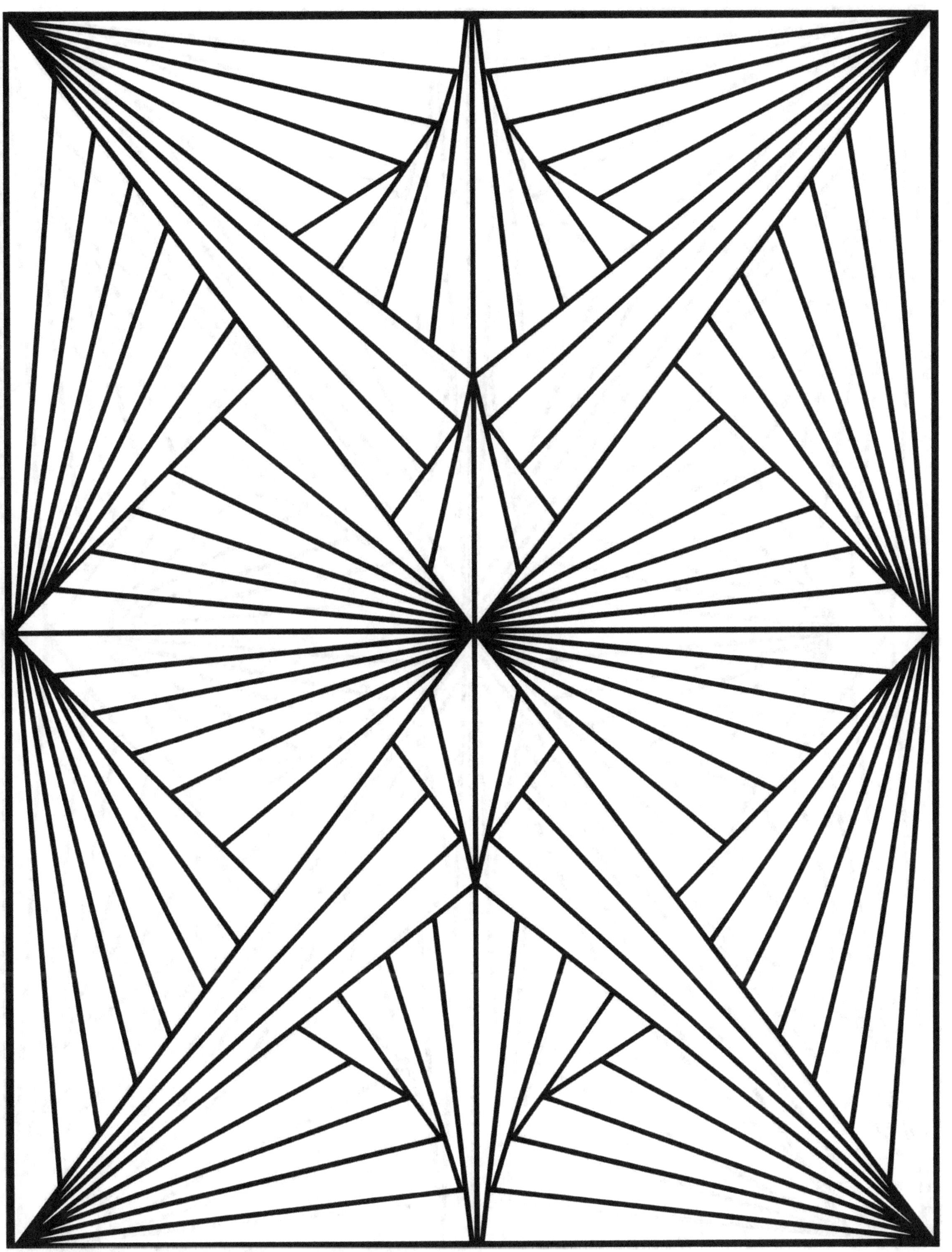

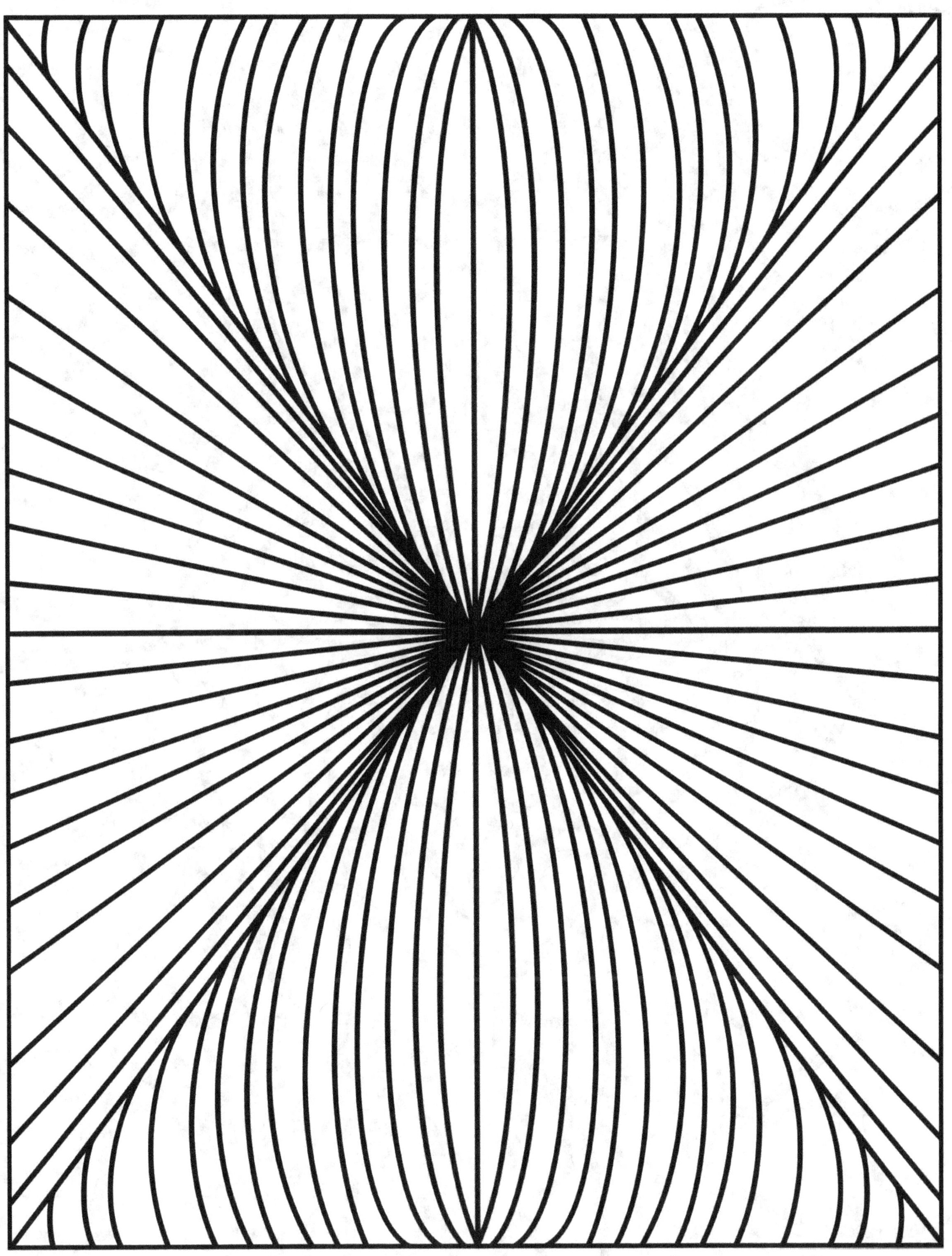

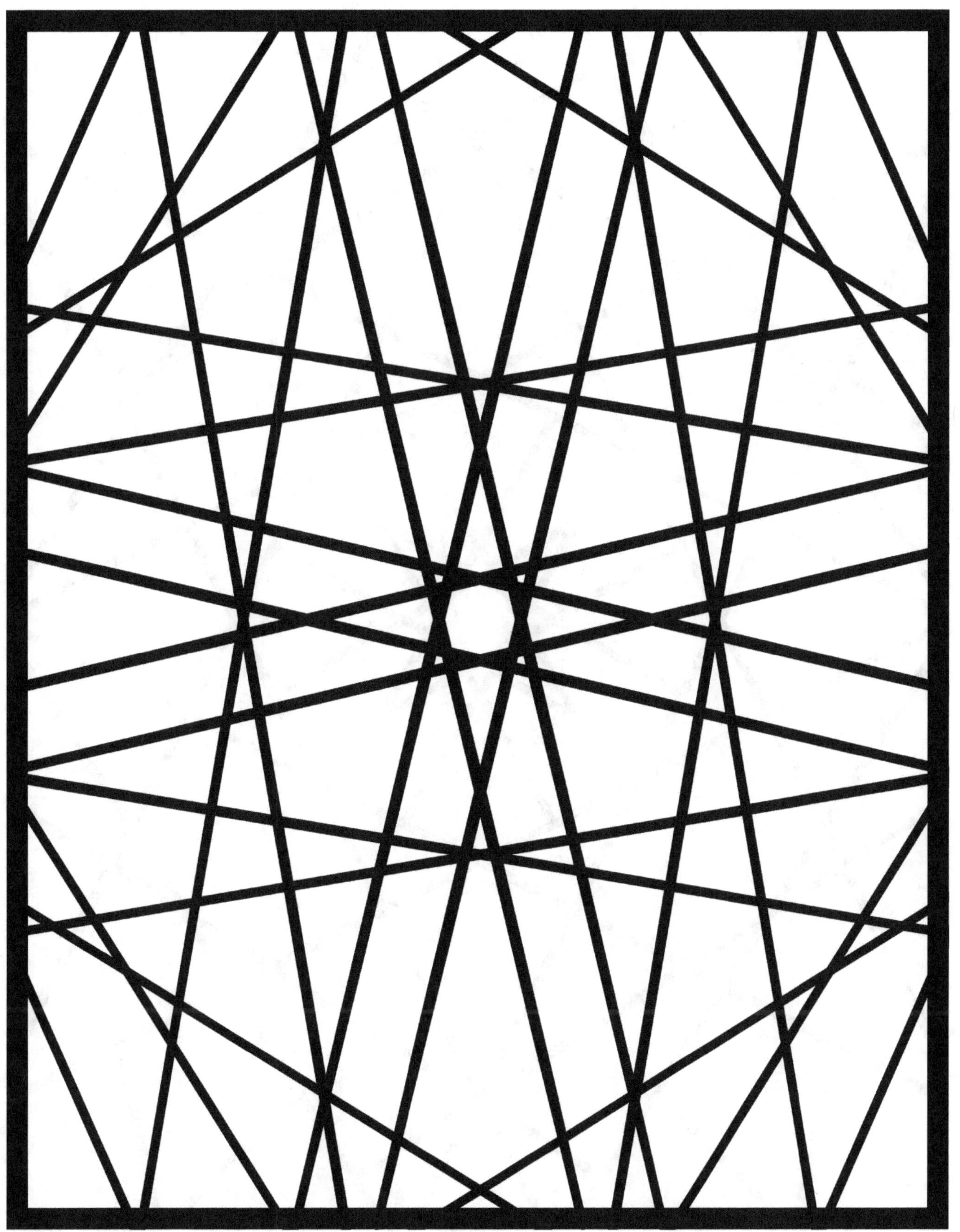

www.ingramcontent.com/pod-product-compliance
Lightning Source LLC
Chambersburg PA
CBHW081419250726
48654CB00013B/1758